"This is *the* book you need if you want to cook with cast iron."
—DIANA HENRY

A humble workhorse used for generations to crisp bacon perfectly and fry chicken, the cast-iron skillet can also turn out tender scones, cakes, and breads. A curious home cook, Charlotte Druckman has figured out every trick for this versatile pan. Heat the skillet for a few minutes, add some butter to sizzle and then brown cheesy arepas, get a crunchy crust on a kimchi-topped hoecake, or blister naan right on the stovetop. Or preheat the pan in the oven and you're ready to bake no-knead pizza, the gooiest sticky buns, and even a cornflake-milk layer cake. With beautiful photographs, tips for seasoning cast iron, and information on collecting vintage pieces, this book makes cooking so much fun that your skillet will never see the cupboard.

"*Stir, Sizzle, Bake* radically reimagines the possibilities for cast iron, and Charlotte is a smart, permissive, and inspiring guide."
—JOHN T. EDGE

STIR,
SIZZLE,
BAKE

CHARLOTTE DRUCKMAN

STIR, SIZZLE, BAKE

RECIPES FOR YOUR
CAST-IRON SKILLET

Photographs by Aubrie Pick

Clarkson Potter/Publishers
NEW YORK

Copyright © 2016 by CHARLOTTE DRUCKMAN
Photographs copyright © 2016 by AUBRIE PICK

Published in the United States by Clarkson
Potter/Publishers, an imprint of the Crown
Publishing Group, a division of Penguin
Random House LLC, New York.
crownpublishing.com | clarksonpotter.com

CLARKSON POTTER is a trademark and
POTTER with colophon is a registered
trademark of Penguin Random House LLC.

Library of Congress Cataloging-in-
    Publication Data
Names: Druckman, Charlotte, author.
Title: Stir, sizzle, bake / Charlotte Druckman.
Description: New York : Clarkson Potter/
    Publishers, [2016] |
Description based on print version record
    and CIP data provided by publisher;
    resource not viewed.
Identifiers: LCCN 2016000893 (print) | LCCN
    2015042045
Subjects: LCSH: Skillet cooking. | Baking. |
    Cast-iron. | LCGFT: Cookbooks.
Classification: LCC TX840.S55 (print) |
    LCC TX840.S55 D78 2016 (ebook) | DDC
    641.7/7—dc23
LC record available at http://lccn.loc.
    gov/2016000893

ISBN 978-0-553-45966-1
eBook ISBN 978-0-553-45967-8

Printed in China

Book and cover design by
Stephanie Huntwork
Cover photograph by Aubrie Pick

10 9 8 7 6 5 4 3 2 1

First Edition

To Judith Jones,
who reminded me that deliciousness
is the goal, but so is having fun
in the process.

And in memory of Gina DePalma,
queen of upside-down cakes and so many
other wonderful things, some related to
baking, and some to being
an outstanding person.

CONTENTS

WHERE IT STARTED

Humankind has been cooking with cast iron for eons, well before there were
cookbooks or even handwritten recipes. It's an enduring material;
it's also a relatively forgiving one. Things have a way of turning
out all right in one of those heavy, searing pans.

Maybe that's because, as I reasoned, you don't see
anything too fancy or delicate being prepared in
them—no foam, no fragile, paper-thin layers, no
custards, no sugar sculpture. Cast-iron skillets are
the workhorses of home cooking. Sweet or savory,
the stuff you fix in them is as accessible as the
pans themselves. That approachability is what
made me take on baking, which, up until then, had
been a source of intimidation.

In the United States, the cast-iron skillet is
typically associated with rustic cooking—outdoorsy
sorts take it camping—and with down-home grub
such as biscuits and cornbread, probably the first
things people think of when you mention "baking"
and "cast iron" in the same sentence. But rustic
needn't be unsophisticated. And biscuits and
cornbread needn't be predictable or adhere to
your grandparents' recipes. You can fool around
with the classics—maybe incorporate Fritos corn
chips into your cornbread, or roasted butternut
squash into your biscuits. And because cast iron is
a globally utilized material, you can—and should—
cull inspiration from multiple locales.

Since I was a little girl, I've been enchanted by
cookbooks. I'd run my hand along the spines on
my parents' kitchen shelves. I'd pick up whatever
volume my mother was cooking from and flip
through it. But for a food writer, having so many

expert opinions at your fingertips can have a
negative effect; it caused me to start second-
guessing myself. Every time I thought about
combining flavors or trying a different cooking
method, I'd question it. My sense of adventure and
creative spirit were gone. Slowly, I stopped cooking.

I missed it, the way I remembered it. Writing a
cookbook dedicated to baking on this metal surface
provided me with an opportunity to sharpen my
own skills, overcome some misgivings I'd had
about certain culinary tasks, and, the real gift, get
my confidence back.

Baking has the reputation of being rigid,
not conducive to improvisation. There are pre-
determined ratios in place—for wet and dry
ingredients and for fat. But having those set
equations frees you up to try out different flavors
and ingredients, so you can make a scone or
pizza your own without turning it into something
unrecognizable or, worse, inedible. With fixed
proportions, you can only go so far before you
will come up against the limits of the baked good
you're trying to produce. The same is true of the
vessel you're cooking in; it provides you with some
fundamental structure. With my trusty pan, I felt
safe to mess around with spices and new types of
flour. I could be more adventurous.

As I developed my recipes, I went back to some of the cookbooks I'd grown up with, and found guidance in a few newer sources. Sometimes, I'd ask chefs to collaborate with me. Working with the masters is always an opportunity to learn, and this time it wasn't at the expense of my self-assurance; it contributed to my improvement and only made me want to spend more time at the stove.

I taught myself to bake so that I could, in turn, teach you. In the process, I reawakened the instinct I used to rely on when I was younger, engaging my imagination and logic to cook things I inherently knew would taste good. I'm convinced we all have that instinct, and my greatest wish is that *Stir, Sizzle, Bake* gets you in touch with yours. Even if your brownies are a bit overcooked, if you have fun making them, and if you start to think about how you might change them next time, maybe adding cinnamon or pretzel dust, I'll have succeeded.

HOW TO USE THIS BOOK

I hope, like a well-used skillet, the copy of the cookbook you are now holding becomes a keepsake, one that you return to again and again. It's intended to be the definitive guide to cooking on cast iron, with a specific emphasis on baking. It's also a solid introduction to baking that can be used as a source of recipes and inspiration for practiced home cooks as well. Those who are new to—or daunted by—cast iron or baking can treat the book as a primer, to be read and worked through in order.

For the first chapter of recipes, "No-Bake Baking," your dough never sees the oven. Each item is cooked on the stovetop. You'll be dealing with a lot of flatbreads. But you'll also get a few not-so-flat rounds out of it. Most of these are easy to make; they're quick and don't require loads of

ingredients. The recipes in the following section, "Easy-Bake Baking," move you into proper baking territory, that is the oven. These may require more prep than the items you made before, but then you can shut the oven door, set your timer, and leave the rest to the machinery. In "On-the-Rise Baking," you get into yeasted dough, kneaded or not. Don't worry. Mostly it requires patience—waiting for a rise, or two, sometimes three.

We've arrived at my favorite chapter, "Make-the-Most-of Baking." I think of these dishes as examples of "baking it forward," because you're using the items you made in the earlier chapters in tandem with other ingredients to deliver stand-alone dishes or, even, meals. Last but not least—this is the category of foodstuff I can't live without—"Condiments." Accompaniments for your breads, most of these, conveniently, are also made in your cast-iron pan.

Skillet Size

Before you get picky about the brand or age of your pan, you should ask yourself what size you need. All the recipes in this book were tested in a Lodge 10¼-inch cast-iron skillet, which is the average diameter of the pan, measured across the top. When you are buying vintage cast-iron skillets, you will see they are numbered according to size. Unfortunately—and confusingly—these numbers do not correspond to any recognizable dimension and were not standardized among manufacturers, so one company's "5" pan may be slightly bigger—or smaller—than another's. Despite these minor discrepancies, you can count on a vintage "8" skillet to be the reliable equivalent of a modern-day 10-inch pan (usually around 10¼ inches, like a Lodge).

ONE PAN, MANY POSSIBILITIES

British food writer Bee Wilson offers a tidy character sketch in her book *Consider the Fork:* "If well seasoned, a cast-iron skillet has excellent nonstick properties, and because it's so heavy, it can withstand the high heat needed for searing." That's a good place to start; still, it only begins to scratch the metal surface.

Though cast-iron skillets take longer to heat than their aluminum or copper counterparts, they amass more thermal energy per pound and are able to get hotter and to stay hotter longer than those others. That intense heat is what makes them so great at searing (everything except fish, with its gentler flesh) and, when it comes to baking, gives you a crunchier, more satisfying crust. The more time you spend with your pan, the more you'll not only begin to appreciate but also to manipulate its strengths to your advantage. You'll even be able to bend some of the alleged rules and understand why some of them can't be broken.

A FEW COOKING RULES

"The most difficult part of cast iron cooking is de-mystifying cast iron cooking."
—Mike Whitehead

1. Hot Is Cool

To reap the best results when baking in your cast-iron pan, almost all of the time—though there are a few exceptions—you have to preheat it. Although you might be tempted to try, you should not place your unbaked dough on a cool pan and then pop it in the oven. It will likely lead to sticking. I learned this the hard way when I tried to bake a Tibetan-style flatbread, on my stovetop, in my unheated cast-iron skillet. My bread was nearly immovable. The cleanup was misery; my cast iron endured, but not without a rather infuriating effort.

Preheating has a few other invaluable benefits. After all my recipe testing and cake eating, what I've learned is that the skillet's concentrated heat can be an asset for many baked goods. The heat provides that extra caramelization on the bottom of a tart shell, bar cookie, or, which I adore, challah; it helps develop the slightly crunchy crust on cornbread, the almost jamlike roasted fruit topping—once flipped—of an upside-down cake, and it puts bubbly blisters on your naan. A dry hot skillet gives you a blackening char; adding fat to the pan is the way to a nut-brown finish.

Placing a small amount of cooking fat down on the hot cast iron and waiting for its temperature to climb not only greases the pan for the optimal "sear," but also helps to build up the skillet's seasoning, which, in turn, protects the pan and increases its nonstick capability. Dave Arnold explains in his indispensable post "Heavy Metal: The Science of Cast Iron Cooking," published on his blog, *Cooking Issues*, that heat plus an unsaturated fat—of the kind found in some vegetable oils—yields a chemical reaction that changes the fat's molecules to form a polymerized coating that repels water, which makes it nonstick. A new skillet (and sometimes an old one) must be properly seasoned before it's used; when the pan's ready for work, by cooking on it with more fat, you will continue to build upon that layer and increase its hydrophobia.

2. Go Ahead and Drop Acid

For a long time, acid (vinegar or citrus) was considered an unconditional no-no for cast iron. But food science expert Harold McGee dispelled this myth when I wanted to find out whether or not I could add a splash of wine to my skillet. "If the pan is well-seasoned, then contact with acids doesn't matter unless it goes on long enough to breach the coating. Brief contact as in deglazing should be fine." So a splash of wine to make a quick sauce of the rendered bits of fat left over from chicken thighs, say, would be hunky-dory. A spritz of lemon juice to bring out the tartness of raspberries being baked into a crisp is A-okay, too. I'm with J. Kenji López-Alt, of *Serious Eats*, who approves of a "short simmer," but suggests you "avoid long-simmered acidic foods, particularly tomato sauce."

Tomatoes are especially problematic. If you've ever prepared a marinara in a cast-iron pot, you may have noticed the sauce tasted bitter or metallic. But you can warm chopped or baby tomatoes in that pan. You can put them in a batter and bake them in the skillet. And, of course, you can pile them, solid or pureed, on top of dough.

3. Soaping Mechanism

Something else that's surprisingly all right for cast iron, if you've treated it as you should, is most modern dish soap. I know, this sounds dangerous: Doesn't Dawn take grease out of your way and isn't that "grease" the barrier that protects your pan and food from each other? Yes and no. Once that "grease" has been polymerized, it's not grease anymore. The Dawns of the world can't hurt it now.

CHOOSING A SKILLET

Something Old

Before you can begin to think about the nitty-gritty of cleaning a cast-iron skillet, you have to own one and might need some help figuring out which to pick. America has a rich legacy in this area. The original makers of "hollow ware," as they called it, were stove companies, cleverly selling vessels to use on the appliances. But not long after the advent of those machines, a number of major foundries positioned themselves as the primary producers of the pots and pans. Wagner (est. 1881), based in Sidney, Ohio, and Griswold (est. 1865), out of Erie, Pennsylvania, were, at one point, the world's largest manufacturers of cast-iron cookware. By 1957, Griswold had been bought out and, soon after, its trademarks and name were purchased by Wagner. In 1969, the rights to both brands were sold to yet another company. That appears to have been the end for Wagner pieces, but those bearing the Griswold mark were being made until 1973.

Today, the market for vintage cast iron is competitive. Collectors are quick to snatch up the valuable items, while the rest of us dilettantes are growing more interested in owning an atavistic pan or two ourselves. It's a seller's market.

In many ways these pans are a lot like old blue jeans; they're American icons that marry form and function. And the same way you can go out and buy yourself some vintage denim, you can find yourself an old skillet, too. Both objects usually require some refurbishment and breaking in. The more expensive ones may have already been cleaned up, as to be ready for use.

If you buy a real fixer-upper, keep in mind, serious effort is required. Grime and oxidation are treatable. A smooth, even-toned surface is ideal. What you should avoid are cracks and craters. If yours is more of a rescue purchase and is covered in egregious amounts of greasy gunk or rusted over, go to a local professional who specializes in cleaning metal objects. There's a shop in New York City called Best Made Company known for its painstakingly crafted axes and knives. The company's product director, Nick Zdon, teaches classes on the restoration of cast-iron skillets and will even strip down and re-season one for you for a fee. Or you can buy an already spruced-up pan from his shop's website, bestmadeco.com.

Other outlets for purchasing vintage vessels include Etsy, where I found a Vermont-based outfit called SeaGlassPrimitives, which strips, cleans, and seasons pans organically. You could just as easily comb flea markets, or, as Sam Sifton suggested in the *New York Times*, stop by "junk shops in towns not known for antiques." He found his "quarry" real cheap—in a church basement in Delaware—and his preferred cast iron–salvation method is a basic elbow-grease application, which, along with re-seasoning—the requisite follow-up— will be addressed in the next chapter.

I'm a big fan of these vintage pieces, and not from a collector's point of view; I love their rich patinas and the fact that, if anything, they improve with age and use. I was listening to *A Taste of the Past,* on Brooklyn's Heritage Radio Network. The show's host, Linda Pelaccio, devoted this particular episode to cast-iron cookware and interviewed two experts, an author/poet named Stacey Harwood and Joel Schiff, a historian who has extensively studied—and collected—holloware. He noted that Griswold's production quality was "excellent," but that most pieces from the early twentieth century— Wagner, Lodge, and Piqua—were "extremely high

> **FUN FACT: Power Tool**
> Did you know you can use your skillet to smash garlic and crush peppercorns?

grade." He advised listeners to "look for things that were finely cast" and described those as "almost lickably smooth; it looks like iron cream when it's cleaned and everything." I nodded with nerdy appreciation at that statement, because those old skillets remind me of cooled, poured molten chocolate, and when I see one, I always have the sudden urge to press my cheek to it. There's nothing like a well-cared-for vintage cast-iron skillet.

Something New

Alternatively, there is nothing wrong with new pans. Lodge cast-iron skillets are ubiquitous, inexpensive, and most definitely serviceable. The company dates back to the tail end of the nineteenth century and, along with Griswold and Wagner, built one of the country's most successful, recognized foundries. It's the only extant brand name of the lot. But the products it puts out today reflect the current technology and economy. These cast-iron pans are preseasoned, allowing you to skip the standard initiation routine. Lodge's website offers general care instructions and walks you through the necessary damage control should your preseasoning begin to peel away. It's easy enough to remedy, and some intrepid project-lovers decide to strip the skillet entirely and start from scratch, sanding down the surface and re-seasoning it.

If you would prefer to invest in a modern-day heirloom and have the budget to spend on one, there's good news: In the past five years, a

A Little History

There is a reason that cast iron has stood the test of time and is used by so many different cultures around the world; it works, and it works hard. The flat circular *comal* on which tortillas are prepared is cast iron. Don't forget griddles, like the Indian *tava* (tawa), or flattop grills, like the Spanish *plancha*. *Panini* pans and their cousins, waffle irons, are also wrought from that metal. The list goes on . . .

When you expose iron oxide to extremely high temperatures and combine it with carbon, you get what's known as pig iron, an impure version of the metal that's hard and brittle. Re-melting this substance yields cast iron. If you dig up examples from the early 1700s, you can see a residual, raised—usually round—"sprue" on the bottom of the vessels, marking the spot where the molten metal had been poured into its mold. By the middle of the eighteenth century, the shape shifted into an extended line, known as a "gate." Either way, these entry points made the pots' bases uneven. This wouldn't have mattered when nestling a kettle into a hearth; once ranges were introduced, though, anything but a flat bottom became problematic.

The method changed to accommodate; a separate entry channel would be attached to the vessel mold so the liquid iron could pass through that "in gate" before filling the hollow cavity. Once the ensuing object had cooled, its attached gate could be hacked off without affecting the smooth, level base. By the end of the nineteenth century, thanks to the Industrial Revolution, there was cast iron aplenty in America: stoves were widely available, and flat-bottomed pans—or skillets—became the norm. Our tendency to refer to them as "frying pans" emphasizes that function. But you can do a lot more with these pans than fry.

couple of artisanal cast-iron outfits—FINEX Cast Iron Cookware Company, in Portland, Oregon, and Borough Furnace, in Syracuse, New York—have begun to manufacture some truly beautiful pans, in smaller quantities, and at higher prices.

A final option is the hybrid enamel-coated cast-iron cookware produced by French companies like Le Creuset and Staub, known for the fun, bright, shiny colors of their exteriors. Both offer skillets whose interiors are coated in dulled black enamel; but I don't recommend them for any recipe that requires you to preheat a dry pan to a high temperature—or, similarly, has you cook something in a dry pan. At intense heat, and without lubrication, that pretty outer layer is prone to cracking. Although I suspect they're better suited to braising, searing, and sautéing than to baking, you should be able to make a number of the recipes in the book with them; I'd avoid the flatbreads, though. I'd also do a slower, lower stovetop preheat. *Best is to follow the respective manufacturer's instructions and warnings.*

CARING FOR YOUR SKILLET

Here are my suggested best practices for skillets, old and new.
It's significantly easier than keeping an apartment plant alive—I've
never been able to do that, but my skillets are just fine, thanks.

SEASONING

Whether you've just discovered a rust- and grime-free skillet in your basement or purchased a new one that needs seasoning, here's what to do:

- Rinse your pan in hot, sudsy water—your preferred dish soap should do. Dry it thoroughly with a kitchen towel. You can also place it on your stovetop over low heat for 5 to 10 minutes, gradually increasing the burner to low-medium, as the metal warms up.

- Add a teaspoon of whatever flavorless unsaturated fat you have on hand—canola, corn, safflower, or vegetable oil all fit the bill—to the skillet. If your pan is hot, handle it carefully, holding it with an oven mitt or pot holder. Using a paper towel, rub the oil over the entire pan, interior and exterior. Blot any residual fat; you want a thin, even coating. Next, place the pan, facedown, in your oven and set the temperature to 450°F to 500°F. It's essential your oven reach a high enough temperature—otherwise, the oil won't completely polymerize and will leave a sticky residue behind.

- When the oven has reached peak heat, leave the skillet in there for another 30 minutes. Turn the oven off and let the pan cool before taking it out. Your skillet should look darker.

- Repeat the above process 3 or 4 more times; when it's well blackened, the pan is ready. Its surface should be substantially resistant to sticking and easier to clean; still, it's important to recognize that, as Dave Arnold points out, "there is no quick way to fully season a cast-iron pan." Your skillet will become increasingly nonstick—and darker and glossier—with regular use.

- If you've bought a preseasoned pan, you should know that its coating is a relatively superficial one; it will protect against rust, but it won't do much to stave off sticking. You don't need to put it through the longer routine previously outlined, but it will benefit from a quick treatment. You should do the aforementioned sudsy rinse, followed by a stovetop dry-off and the oil rub. You don't need to put the skillet in the oven. It's good to go.

Some extra essentials for your cast iron:
- Flaxseed oil (such as Barlean's)
- Silicone oven mitt (such as OXO)
- Tawashi palm scrubber (such as one sold at Korin)

PREHEATING

Because cast iron is slower to heat and does so unevenly, preheating, essential for searing, is also almost always recommended for frying, roasting, and baking. You can do this in your oven or, when you're doing a stovetop preparation, on a burner. Ideally, it should be done gradually. This is easy enough in your oven—just put the pan in there while you preheat the appliance.

It's a little more involved on the stovetop, but not much: Start the skillet over low heat, incrementally increasing that to whatever your desired cooking temperature is. Make sure you place the pan an inch or two off center and rotate it every couple of minutes, so it circles the heat source; this keeps the middle of the skillet from receiving all that direct heat and developing a hot spot. J. Kenji López-Alt recommends you give this a solid 10 minutes. If you think your pan is too hot for the pending task—making naan (page 22), for example—lower the heat, and remember that cast iron is slower to register temperature adjustments.

CLEANING

When I asked Mike Whitehead, founder of FINEX Cast Iron Cookware Company, what he'd tell someone who said she didn't want to get started with cast iron because it's too difficult to clean, he replied, "Get over it and start living." I couldn't have put it better myself. That said, there are a few easy tricks.

Always wash your pan by hand; never put it in the dishwasher. When you rinse your pan after cooking in it, with or without soap, match the water temperature accordingly (don't introduce your hot skillet to a rush of cold liquid). A soft-bristled brush or a Japanese *tawashi* (a vegetable scrub brush) will help remove any minor debris without endangering the seasoning.

If you're faced with more substantial sticking, you can boil water in your skillet and use a wooden spatula to scrape the caked-on particles off the pan. Or go on and bust out your metal spatula: Dave Arnold discovered that "the gentle scraping of metal along the bottom of the pan while cooking helps to even out the surface of the seasoning and make it more durable, not less."

A natural exfoliant, kosher salt is another excellent option for removing the clingier bits. Sprinkle enough of it on your skillet to cover the interior, then, using a dampened paper towel, or, as I've seen done, the cut side of a halved potato, start scrubbing. The salt will get dirty as it lifts the gunk off your pan. (Repeat the process if necessary, rinsing the salt out before applying more.) When the surface is clear, rinse the dirty salt out.

After cleaning your pan, dry it thoroughly by hand and on the stove, over low heat, for a few minutes. Finally, rub it down with a teaspoon of the cooking oil of your choice. (I use flaxseed.) Make sure you follow this quick last step every time. It prevents rust. So does removing your baked items from your skillet as soon they're cooled and storing them elsewhere because, as Mike Whitehead notes, "depending on how seasoned your cookware is, the food might be damp enough to cause some slight corrosion." Don't leave your pan sitting under running water for a long period of time or soak it, either.

STORING

If you've got the kitchen wall space to hang your skillet, do it. That way it's always within reach. It's weightier than most pans, so make sure it's well supported. My 10-inch skillet stays on my stove because it's the one I cook in most often, and I use it a lot. The rest of my cast-iron pans are kept in a dry space—I nest them in my cupboard, one inside the other, and place a piece of paper towel between each to protect its surface from rust or dust.

REMOVING RUST

No matter how hard you try, it's likely that at some point you'll find rust on your cast iron. You have not failed, and your skillet is not a goner. This is when you "get out the steel wool"—*not* the soap-filled kind, the plain stuff. When you use an abrasive on cast iron, you will strip it of any rust, which is great; you will also strip it of its seasoning. You'll simply have to start over, as though you'd just procured your pan, and re-season it. Take it from the top!

Oil Spill

You'll know if you've overoiled your pan, because it will be noticeably tacky just like it would be if you didn't season it at a high enough temperature. Or else you'll start to notice black flecks on your food. Dave Arnold explains: "The oil polymer on a well-used piece of cast iron is built of many thin layers deposited over time. Thick layers can flake off in large pieces. Thin layers will remain adhered to the pan and will slough off microscopically."

If your pan shows these signs, get your steel wool out and re-season it. And if you need to correct a neglected or seriously botched seasoning job, and you've got the moxie to do it, Dave Arnold says you can put your skillet in your oven and turn on the self-clean cycle, or place it in your fireplace. Somewhere near 800°F, the offending coating will be incinerated, and its ashes are all that's left of it.

NO-BAKE BAKING

Opposite: Galette with Picklish Plums, page 61

BLISTERED PIZZA NAAN

makes 10 flatbreads

1 cup unbleached all-purpose
    flour, plus more for dusting
1 cup whole-wheat flour
¾ cup spelt flour
1 teaspoon kosher salt
½ teaspoon baking powder

2 tablespoons za'atar
1 (16-ounce) container labneh
    (1⅔ packed cups), or 1⅓ cups
    plain low-fat or regular kefir
    yogurt drink (see Note)

⅓ cup extra-virgin olive oil
1½ teaspoons flake salt, for
    garnish

Sometimes, you're lucky enough to know you're experiencing a defining moment as it takes place. Maybe you're in your kitchen, rolling out a circle of dough, and then placing it in the pan and watching the disc bubble up, blister, and become bread right before your eyes. Then you tear into the probably-too-hot-but-who-cares flatbread, and you think: *I did it! I made naan, from scratch, for the first time . . . and it's holy-mackerel delicious.*

Maybe for you, it was something else. For me, though, this naan moment was real. So I've got to thank chef Caroline Fidanza of the Brooklyn sandwich shop Saltie, whose recipe I was testing that day in my kitchen. While I kept her ratio of dry-to-wet ingredients and cooking method, I added whole-wheat to the mix and opted for labneh as my wet ingredient, which, although referred to as a soft cheese, is more like an extra-thick yogurt. To give my naan some New York City personality and flavor—by way of the Middle East—I threw za'atar into my dough. When you bite into the blistered, hot bread, it's as though you're eating a NYC slice, without the sauce, cheese, or mess.

1 In a large bowl, whisk together the flours, kosher salt, baking powder, and za'atar. Using a wooden spoon, stir the labneh into the dry ingredients. When the dough becomes too stiff to mix with a spoon, dust your hands with flour and begin to knead the dough in the bowl, continuing until the ingredients are thoroughly combined. Cover the bowl with plastic wrap and let it ferment in the refrigerator for at least 1 hour and up to 2 days.

2 Preheat a 10-inch cast-iron skillet on the stovetop, gradually raising the heat from low to medium-high, so it gets very hot. Meanwhile, shape the dough: Dust your work surface liberally with flour (make sure you have enough on hand as you go, because the dough will be very sticky). Shape the dough into 10 balls, 3 to 3½-inches in diameter. Use a floured rolling pin to roll each ball into a circle about 6 inches in diameter. Stack the circles as you go, separating them with wax paper to prevent them from sticking together.

3 Once the skillet is smoking, coat it with 1 tablespoon of the oil. Pick up a dough circle, stretch it out a bit more, shake off any excess flour, and place it in the skillet. Cook the naan for 1 to 2 minutes, until it starts to bubble. Drizzle ½ teaspoon of the oil over the top of the naan, then use tongs to flip it. Cook the naan for 1 to 2 minutes more, until its underside is blistered and speckled with brown spots and there is no visible raw flour. (If you're unsure whether it's ready, watch the flatbread's edges; when they start to curl up and brown, like a pancake, it's done.) If the naan is getting too crispy or starting to burn, reduce the heat to medium.

4 Repeat with the remaining dough, adding 1 teaspoon of oil to the pan between one naan and the next. Stack the finished flatbreads on a plate as you go to keep them warm, sprinkling each with a pinch of flake salt.

5 The naan should be eaten warm. Wrapped in plastic, it will keep at room temperature for up to 2 days. Before serving, reheat it in a 350°F oven until it's warmed through.

NOTE Labneh is a strained yogurt, a Middle Eastern fermented milk product. If you can't find labneh, you can replace it with kefir, which is now available in major supermarket chains across the country, and has a similar texture and acidic punch.

GARLIC ROTI

makes 10 flatbreads

20 garlic cloves

1¼ pounds (5 sticks) plus
3 tablespoons unsalted butter

1½ cups kamut flour, plus more
for dusting (see Note)

1¼ teaspoons table or fine
sea salt

¾ cup warm water, plus more
as needed

2 tablespoons chopped fresh basil

Sugar (optional)

1½ teaspoons flake salt,
for garnish

One night I stopped by a friend's dinner party in Brooklyn and found food editor Alison Roman making a distractingly aromatic naan that channeled her love of garlic bread. I immediately wanted to do the same. She told me she incorporated the allium into the dough, but I never had a chance to ask her how, or to taste the results, because I had to leave for another dinner.

A few months later, I tested a recipe from San Francisco chef Brandon Jew that included a garlic purée unlike anything I'd ever had—silky smooth, almost like finessed mashed potatoes in texture. In his technique, the garlic is cooked low and slow in enough oil to cover, yielding a result that's better even than roasted garlic. For my roti, I use butter instead of oil to create a garlicky ghee that goes into the dough and is brushed onto the roti. You could sprinkle the bread with sea salt and be more than satisfied. But the real *WHOA* effect hits if, right before you take your first bite, you spread a purée made with that butter-braised garlic directly on the warm, floppy bread.

1 Place the garlic and butter in a medium saucepan and bring to a simmer over medium-low heat. Slowly simmer the mixture, skimming the white foam off the top as you go, until the melted butter takes on a clear, deeper, more concentrated golden hue and ceases to sputter, the milk solids at the bottom of the pan begin to brown, and the garlic cloves are soft enough to mash with a spoon with very little pressure. This may take up to 1½ hours.

2 Strain the ghee into a storage container, discarding any sediment and reserving the garlic cloves in a separate container. You should have at least 2 cups of ghee. Set aside to cool.

3 Sift the kamut and 1 teaspoon of the table salt together into a large bowl. Add 2 tablespoons of the cooled ghee and use your fingers to incorporate it into the dry ingredients, rubbing it through the flour so it's evenly distributed. Slowly add the water, using your

hand to work it in, until the dough comes together in a ball. I use the swirl-n-grab method: one hand sifts through and grabs the contents of the bowl in a circular motion while the other slowly pours in the water. You should find yourself grabbing larger and larger clumps as the dough comes together.

4   Gather the dough into a ball and begin kneading it; if it needs more water, add it by the teaspoon, adding less than you think is necessary so you don't overdo it. (If you add too much, and the dough becomes wet, coat your hands with the flour and knead it into the dough.) Knead the dough for about 7 minutes, until your bowl and hands are free of any dough or flour and the dough itself is smooth and supple. Cover the bowl with a damp kitchen towel and set aside to rest for 30 minutes.

5   Meanwhile, purée the cooked garlic in a food processor, incorporating 1 teaspoon of water to stabilize the emulsion. With the motor running, drizzle in ¼ cup of the ghee, little by little, until combined. (Alternatively, you can purée the garlic in a bowl using a fork, then whisk in the ghee.) Transfer the purée to a bowl and season with the remaining ¼ teaspoon table salt. Add the basil and stir to combine. Taste the purée: if you prefer a milder garlic flavor or your garlic has any bitterness, stir in a small amount (about ¼ teaspoon) of sugar. Give it another taste, adjusting the seasonings as needed. Set it aside and keep warm.

6   Preheat a 10-inch cast-iron skillet on the stovetop, gradually raising the heat from low to medium-high, so it gets very hot. Meanwhile, shape the rotis: Divide the dough into 10 equal portions and, using your palms, roll each into a ball. Cover the dough balls with a damp cloth. Working one at a time and keeping the others covered, place a ball on a well-floured work surface and, with a rolling pin, roll it out into a small circle. Flip it over and roll it a bit more, repeating this action until you have a thin 6-inch disc.

7   Place the rolled-out dough on the hot skillet. After a few seconds, when you start to see the dough bubble up, use the back of a spoon or a pastry brush to gently swipe ¼ teaspoon of the ghee on its surface. Flip it over and swipe more ghee onto the other side. Flip the dough again and cook for 1 to 2 minutes. Meanwhile, roll out your next ball of dough, making sure to liberally dust your work surface with flour as you go.

8   Flip the roti in the skillet and give it another 1 to 2 minutes. Use your pastry brush to lightly apply pressure when it puffs up, or else try running the back of your spoon over the roti a few times as it cooks to encourage the bread to rise and bubble.

9   When both sides are nicely speckled with brown spots, transfer the roti to a napkin-lined basket or deep serving platter, smear another ½ teaspoon of the ghee over the top, sprinkle with a pinch of the flake salt, and

(RECIPE CONTINUES)

cover it with a kitchen towel to keep it warm and prevent it from drying out.

10   Repeat with the remaining dough. You will need to add extra ghee to the skillet a few times throughout the course of cooking the rotis. If the skillet starts to overheat and smoke or the rotis burn, reduce the heat to medium and add ¼ teaspoon of ghee to the pan before adding the next disc of dough.

11   Serve the rotis hot; you can slather each one with ½ teaspoon of the garlic-basil purée before serving, or serve the purée on the side as a condiment. Though they're best eaten right away, you can stack the rotis, separated by wax paper, wrap them in aluminum foil, and refrigerate them for up to a day or freeze them for up to 3 months. Reheat them in the foil at 425°F for 15 to 20 minutes. Any unused ghee will keep in a sealed container in a dry, cool place for up to 2 months. Stored in a sealed container, the garlic purée will keep in the refrigerator for 3 days.

> **NOTE**   Similar to *atta*, the durum wheat flour traditionally used for roti, ancient kamut, has a notably buttery character, which is even more appropriate for this particular recipe.

On the Grind

Toasting and grinding your own spices, seeds, and nuts make a huge difference in the quality and intensity of flavor in your baked goods. You can toast them right in your cast-iron skillet. Preheat the pan on the stovetop, gradually raising the heat from low to medium-high. Once the pan is hot, pour the seeds and/or spices in, shaking the pan so they spread out and don't stick together. Toast them, shaking the skillet every few seconds, until they begin to brown and release their oils, emitting a concentrated, heady smell.

Time will vary depending on the quantity and size of the items and on how brown you like them to get. When they begin to release their aroma, they're ready. If you like a more deeply toasted result, wait for that scent to intensify, but watch them carefully so they don't burn, which can happen quickly. For a sense of timing, follow the chart below.

WHAT TO TOAST	HOW LONG
2 tablespoons Sichuan peppercorns	3 minutes
½ teaspoon sesame seeds	2–3 minutes
1 teaspoon cumin seeds	2 minutes
¼ cup pumpkin seeds	3 minutes
1 teaspoon ground cardamom pods	3 minutes
¼ cup pine nuts	3 minutes
2 cups cashew nuts	4–5 minutes

EXTRA-COCONUTTY ROTI

makes about a dozen flatbreads

1½ cups fresh or frozen grated unsweetened coconut (see Note)

1 cup unbleached all-purpose flour

1 cup spelt flour

1 teaspoon salt

½ teaspoon ground freshly toasted green cardamom pods or store-bought ground cardamom (see page 26)

1½ cups warm water

2 tablespoons coconut oil

Coconut butter, for serving

Maple syrup, for serving (optional)

This Sri Lankan breakfast skillet bread, which is typically served with a chile paste or coconut sambal (a spiced relish), has a few alterations. First, for some extra nuttiness, I substitute spelt for half the standard white flour. Next, I add some cardamom to the batter; it's irresistible when paired with coconut. I also swipe coconut butter on the hot rounds when they come off the skillet. And then I eat them—just so. Keep in mind that this is an extremely thick batter. Some might even call it a dough, although it would be a very wet one. Don't let these categories trip you up. If you do, you might prevent yourself from pouring a bit of maple syrup over the rotis and eating them like pancakes, American style. That would be a shame.

1   Preheat a 10-inch cast-iron skillet on the stovetop, gradually raising the heat from low to medium so it gets very hot. Meanwhile, in a medium bowl, whisk together the coconut, flours, salt, and cardamom. Form a well in the center of the dry ingredients and add the warm water. Using a wooden spoon, stir until a thick, coarse batter forms.

2   Melt 2 teaspoons of the coconut oil in the hot skillet and tilt to coat. Using a tablespoon or medium cookie scoop, drop 4 heaping portions of batter into the pan. Wait a few seconds for the batter to become spreadable, then flatten each glob of batter with a spatula to form discs about 3 inches in diameter and ¼ inch thick.

3   Cook the rotis for about 4 minutes on the first side, until toasty brown. Flip them over and rotate them 180 degrees clockwise, for more even doneness. Cook them for 3 minutes more so both sides are equally browned.

4   Transfer the rotis to a serving plate. While they're still hot, spread coconut butter on each. Repeat with the rest of the batter. Eat them right away, with maple syrup, if desired.

> **NOTE**   Most Asian groceries have grated coconut in the freezer section. Bring it to room temperature before using it in this recipe.

MOROCCAN M'SMEN WITH RAS EL HANOUT

makes 12 flatbreads

1¼ cups unbleached all-purpose flour

1¼ cups semolina flour, plus more for sprinkling

1 tablespoon ras el hanout

1½ teaspoons baking powder

1 teaspoon salt

1 large egg

¾ cup warm water

Canola oil

5 tablespoons butter, preferably goat butter (see Note), melted

This Moroccan pancake is a more challenging stovetop bread to make because it's one of the thinnest. A cross between a crepe and a flatbread, *m'smen* reminds me of filo dough in terms of handling. Greasing your palms—and the dough—is key. Of course, when you're starting out, no one will care if you make them a little thicker. Either way, it's going to be delicious, and I've made a few adjustments to guarantee as much, like the addition of *ras el hanout*. I suspect this Moroccan spice blend, comprised of allspice, possibly aphrodisiacal ash berries, potentially toxic belladonna leaves, and a myriad of other aromatics, may have been used by the witches in *Macbeth*. It's certainly cast its spell on me.

1   In the bowl of a stand mixer, using a whisk, stir together the flours, ras el hanout, baking powder, and salt. Add the egg. Fit the bowl on the mixer and, using the dough hook, mix the ingredients at medium-low speed. With the mixer running, gradually add the water until a ball of dough forms. It shouldn't be sticky or too moist. If necessary, add more semolina flour, 1 tablespoon, or less, at a time. Continue to mix the dough for about

8 minutes more, or until it is very smooth, soft, and elastic. (You can do this by hand if you don't have a stand mixer, but note that the dough may seem as if it doesn't have enough moisture to come together at first. Don't worry—once you add the very last bit of water, it should come out just right.)

2   Turn the dough out onto an oiled, nonporous work surface (like a smooth countertop, Silpat mat, or baking sheet). Grease your hands and the dough with the oil, too. Using either your thumb and index finger in a grasping-and-squeezing motion or a bench scraper, divide the dough evenly into 12 pieces, each about 1½ inches in diameter. Shape the pieces into tight balls the size of a walnut or tiny tangerine and place them on an oiled baking sheet. Coat each ball with more oil and cover them with aluminum foil or a kitchen towel.

3   Coat your hands with more oil. Working one at a time and keeping the others covered,

(RECIPE CONTINUES)

place a dough ball on the greased work surface. Pat the ball into a disc, and, using the top of your palm and heel of your hand, massage the dough into a large, flat circle, pushing outward so it gets thinner and thinner. Continue to push and flatten—being careful to avoid tears—until you've got an evenly paper-thin, nearly transparent sheet of dough about 7 inches in diameter (or 9 inches, if you're a more experienced dough-handler). Brush the dough with some of the melted butter and sprinkle it with semolina flour.

4   Fold the top and bottom edges of the dough toward the center, one on top of the other, to form a long rectangle that resembles a folded crepe. Brush the dough with butter, then fold the right and left edges toward the center, one on top of the other, to form a 3-inch square. Pat the packet and brush it with more butter. Set the packet aside on an oiled pan. Repeat with the remaining dough. Cover the packets again, as before, and let them rest for 15 minutes.

5   Preheat a 10-inch cast-iron skillet on the stovetop, gradually raising the heat from low to medium.

6   Working with your hands on your oiled work surface, using the same massaging technique as above, press one of the dough packets out into a 6-inch square. Carefully lift the square with your fingers, transfer it to the hot skillet, and cook for about 3 minutes per side, or until the bread is speckled and golden brown and its center has puffed a bit.

If the dough begins to puff too much, press it down with a spatula. Transfer the finished m'smen to a rack to cool and repeat with the remaining packets.

7   When you're ready to eat them, reheat the m'smen in a hot, dry skillet. Alternatively, eat them immediately when they come off the pan. Enjoy them with melted butter and honey, or, as I do, serve them with goat cheese, honey, and coarsely chopped oil-cured black Moroccan olives. If you love ras el hanout as much as I, you can sprinkle some more of that over the top, too.

8   Wrapped individually in aluminum foil, the m'smen can be kept in the refrigerator for a couple of days or in the freezer for up to a month.

NOTE   *Smen*, a fermented clarified, cultured butter, is a foundation of Moroccan cuisine. Sour and funky, it is produced by using butter made—most often—from goat and/or sheep milk. I wanted to incorporate it into this flatbread, but it's a hard ingredient to come by. Instead, I recommend goat butter, which you can find in local food specialty shops, including Whole Foods. It has a gamy richness that imparts a *smen*-esque depth. Regular unsalted butter is fine, but to get more flavor from it, try clarifying it first. Clarified butter is the result of cooking the fat to separate—and remove—its solids and water from its butterfat. For maximum pungency, clarify your goat butter.

"LAUGHSE"

makes 10 flatbreads

2 cups Simon Hopkinson's
  Saffron Mashed Potatoes
  (recipe follows), chilled
  overnight or for up to 3 days

1½ to 1⅞ cups all-purpose flour,
  plus more for dusting
1 teaspoon unsalted butter, plus
  more as needed

Flake salt, for serving (optional)

In Norway, making this giant, crepe-thin, potato-based flatbread is an art, passed down and practiced generationally. Sam Sifton included a bare-bones recipe in a Thanksgiving story in the *New York Times*, providing alternative instructions for those who do not have the designated griddle, the square-cut grooved wooden rolling pin, or the thin paddle designed for transferring the slender wafer of dough from the countertop to the pan. I doubt I ever would have attempted this thing if not for one knee-weakening temptation: food writer Simon Hopkinson's Saffron Mashed Potatoes.

With a little tweaking, I was able to mesh Simon's recipe and Sam's, and the result? Think *saffronated*, browned mashed potatoes. Most important, I acknowledged the impossibility of perfection and focused, instead, on the pleasure in the process and the deliciousness to come. My lefse, which I affectionately refer to as *LAUGH-se* for their complete lack of legitimacy or tidiness, wins, hands down, in the flavor category. They aren't intended to be authentic; they're for people like me who know not of fjords and aren't afraid of trying something new and different.

1   In a large bowl, using a wooden spoon, mix the mashed potatoes with 1 cup of the flour. Stir until the flour has been absorbed into the potatoes before adding another ½ cup of the flour. The mixture will show dry, crumbly streaks that are then incorporated and leave a mass of thicker mashed potatoes in their wake. Add another ¼ cup of flour to make the mixture more doughlike. Add more flour by the tablespoon, as needed, until the mixture becomes a workable dough.

2   Turn out the dough onto a lightly floured work surface and knead it a few times to smooth it. Using your hands, roll it into a thick log and then, using a bench scraper or sharp knife, divide it into 10 portions. Roll the pieces of dough between your palms to form small balls and place them on one large or two medium plates. Cover the plate(s) with plastic wrap and refrigerate for 1 hour.

3   Ten minutes before you plan to start cooking the flatbreads, preheat a 10-inch cast-iron skillet on the stovetop, gradually raising the heat from low to medium-high.

(RECIPE CONTINUES)

4   Dust your work surface with flour and pour some more into a small bowl. Remove one ball of dough from the refrigerator and toss it in the bowl to coat it with flour. Shake off any excess and set the ball on your work surface. Using the heel of your hand, flatten the dough into a thick disc. Sprinkle both sides with more flour.

5   Dust your rolling pin with flour and gently and slowly begin to roll out the disc from the center, pushing out in one or two directions a couple of times before flipping the dough over and rotating it. Repeat the rolling gesture a few times, carefully spreading the dough out in a circle as you continue to flip and rotate. You may need to sprinkle more flour on the dough or your rolling pin as you go.

6   Once the dough is as thin as possible (not so thin that it's tearing or that you can't move it), shake off any excess flour and drape it over the rolling pin. This will become easier with practice.

7   Melt the butter in the hot skillet. Gently lay the dough in the pan and cook for about 2 minutes, until the bottom is flecked with brown. Using a thin spatula, flip the dough and cook for 2 minutes on the second side. Transfer the lefse to a plate and cover with a clean kitchen towel.

8   Repeat with the remaining dough. After you flip the flatbread in the skillet to cook the second side, take another dough ball from the refrigerator and roll it out, so it's ready to go into the skillet immediately after the first is done. If the flatbread begins to stick to the pan, melt a small pat of butter in the skillet and blot away the excess with a paper towel so the pan is just coated with fat. You may need to do this after every two to three rounds. If the pan gets too hot, reduce the heat to medium. Keep the finished flatbreads under the kitchen towel so they stay warm and don't dry out.

9   Lefse—and "laughse"—are best enjoyed warm. Roll them up and eat them as is, with or without a pinch of salt, or spread on some orange marmalade, tomato jam, or romesco sauce first. Try experimenting with your own toppings.

10 Leftover lefse can be stacked, separated by wax paper, wrapped in aluminum foil, and refrigerated for up to a week or frozen for several months. Thaw at room temperature (if frozen), and reheat, still wrapped in the foil, in the oven at 350°F for 10 minutes before serving.

(RECIPE CONTINUES)

SIMON HOPKINSON'S SAFFRON MASHED POTATOES

serves 4

2 pounds russet or Yukon Gold potatoes, peeled and
   cut into chunks (about 6 heaping cups)

2 teaspoons salt

1 teaspoon saffron threads (if you love saffron,
   make it a heaping teaspoon)

1 large garlic clove, finely chopped

¾ cup plus 2 tablespoons whole milk

¾ cup plus 2 tablespoons extra-virgin olive oil

1 Put the potatoes in a medium-large
   saucepan. Add enough cold water to cover
   them by 1 inch and 1 teaspoon of the salt.
   Bring to a boil over high heat. Once the water
   comes to a boil, cook the potatoes for 10 to
   15 minutes, until fork-tender.

2 Meanwhile, in a small saucepan, combine
   the saffron, garlic, and milk and heat over
   medium-low heat just until the edges of the
   liquid start to bubble, about 10 minutes; do
   not scald the milk. Turn off the heat, cover
   the saucepan, and let the flavors infuse for
   10 minutes. Add the olive oil to the milk
   infusion and gently reheat over low heat.

3 Drain the potatoes and pass them through
   a food mill into the bowl of a stand mixer.
   Fit the mixer with the paddle and with the
   mixer running on low-medium speed, slowly
   stream in the infused milk mixture and whip
   until the potatoes are smooth. (If you don't
   have a stand mixer, you can do this in a large
   bowl with a whisk; just make sure to whisk
   the potatoes until smooth.)

4 Stir in the remaining 1 teaspoon salt. Taste
   and season with more salt, if needed. Set the
   purée in a warm place for about 30 minutes
   to fully develop the saffron flavor. If using for
   the lefse (page 31), refrigerate the mashed
   potatoes overnight or for up to 3 days; but
   if you haven't the willpower to resist, spoon
   them into a serving bowl or onto 4 plates and
   dig in.

SICHUAN PEPPER–SCALLION FLATBREAD

makes 8 rounds

3 cups unbleached all-purpose
flour, plus more for dusting
2 tablespoons shiitake powder
(see Notes, optional)
2 teaspoons baking powder
1 teaspoon salt
½ cup boiling water

½ cup plus 2 tablespoons cold
water
1 tablespoon plus 1 teaspoon
toasted sesame oil
2 teaspoons Sichuan
peppercorns, toasted and
ground (see page 26)

1 cup finely chopped scallions
(white and light green parts)
Peanut oil, for cooking
Shaoxing-Butter Sauce, warm,
for serving (recipe follows;
optional)
Flake salt, for sprinkling (optional)
Soy sauce, for dipping (optional)

I've seen plenty of crispy, flaky, slightly greasy (winningly so, usually) scallion pancakes thanks to years of eating Chinese-American food in New York City and beyond. Though they're listed as "pancakes" on menus, they're not made from a batter; they're made from a laminated dough, meaning each thin stratum is separated by a layer of fat—in this case, oil. And if we're being semantically responsible, since the dough is unleavened, we have to acknowledge that a scallion pancake is, in fact, a flatbread.

I added a secret weapon: a powder made of dried shiitake mushrooms, which lends a subtle, meaty boost. There's more pepper in my dough, too. I love those dark-dusty-rose-colored buds, with their mild citrus flavor that gives way to a pins-and-needles tingling on the tongue. These tweaks give the otherwise relatively bland flour-and-water base enough presence to make it worthwhile. And it gets even better when brushed with a buttery, gingery Shaoxing wine sauce. Is it a flatbread, or is it a pancake? Does it matter?

1   **Start the dough:** Place the flour, shiitake powder (if using), baking powder, and salt in a food processor and pulse a few times to combine. With the motor running, add the boiling water through the feed tube in a thin stream, followed immediately by the cold water. Process for 1 to 2 minutes, until the dough forms a rough ball. Process for another minute. Turn out the dough onto a lightly floured work surface and knead it for 30 seconds to 1 minute, so it's smooth and forms a more compact ball. Cover it with plastic wrap and set it aside for 15 minutes.

2   **Finish the dough:** Using a bench scraper, divide the dough into 8 equal pieces. Cover them with plastic wrap. Working with one at a time and keeping the others covered, place one piece of the dough on a lightly floured work surface and shape it into a ball. Using a lightly floured rolling pin, flatten it into an 8-inch-wide disc.

(RECIPE CONTINUES)

NOTES

- To make the dough in advance, refrigerate the prepared rounds in plastic wrap until the next day. Wait until right before you start cooking the dough to make the sauce.

- Make the shiitake powder with 1 (1-ounce) package dried shiitake mushrooms (about 15). Place the dried mushrooms in a food processer and run the machine until they're ground into a fine dust, up to 5 minutes. Store the powder in a sealed container at room temperature for up to a year.

3   Sprinkle ½ teaspoon of the sesame oil over the flattened dough, followed by ⅛ to ¼ teaspoon of the Sichuan pepper, according to your heat preference. Using your fingertip, evenly spread them together over the dough's surface. Sprinkle 2 tablespoons of the scallions over the dough, leaving a bit of room around the edges.

4   As tightly as possible, roll the dough up like a jellyroll to form a cigar-shaped tube. Coil the tube into a tight spiral, making sure the tail end is sealed and tucked in. Flatten the coil with your palm. Using a rolling pin, gently roll the coil out until it's between 6 and 7 inches wide and around ¼ inch thick. (If any scallions burst through the dough, use your fingers to repair holes and incorporate the scallions back into the dough.)

5   Preheat a 10-inch cast-iron skillet on the stovetop, gradually increasing the heat from low to medium while you begin to roll out the second piece of dough. When the skillet is hot, add the peanut oil: For a chewy, doughy flatbread, add 1 teaspoon peanut oil and tilt to coat. For a crispy, shallow-fried pancake, add 2½ tablespoons peanut oil instead.

6   Brush any excess flour off the first dough round and place it in the skillet. Cook for 4 minutes, until the underside is toasted and covered with brown spots with no raw flour visible (if it's a thinner disc, check it after 3 minutes). Flip the flatbread over and cook for 4 minutes more, until the second side resembles the first. Transfer the flatbread to a rack to cool slightly, then wrap it in a kitchen towel so it stays soft.

7   Repeat with the remaining dough. While one round is in the pan cooking, shape and fill another, keeping your eye on the dough in the skillet as you work. Continue to flour your work surface and rolling pin as you go, and add 1 teaspoon of peanut oil to the skillet before you cook each flatbread.

8   Serve immediately. (Alternatively, you can keep them in the warming drawer of an oven or in an oven set to 200°F.) Brush the flatbreads with the warm Shaoxing-Butter Sauce, whisking it first to incorporate again. If you are skipping the sauce, sprinkle the flatbreads with flake salt as soon as you take them out of the pan. You can also dip them in soy sauce.

SHAOXING-BUTTER SAUCE
makes approximately ½ cup

4 tablespoons (½ stick) unsalted butter
1½ tablespoons Shaoxing cooking wine or medium-dry sherry
1 tablespoon soy sauce
1 (1-inch) knob fresh ginger, peeled and thinly sliced

In a small saucepan, melt the butter over medium-low heat. Reduce the heat to low and whisk in the wine and soy sauce. Add the ginger and bring the sauce to a simmer, increasing the heat to medium-low, if necessary. Reduce the heat to very low to infuse the sauce with the ginger's flavor and keep the sauce warm while you make the flatbreads.

THE IRISH SODA FARLS THAT STARTED IT ALL

makes 1 loaf

2½ cups plus 1 tablespoon all-purpose flour, plus more for dusting (see Note)

1¼ teaspoons baking soda

1¼ teaspoons sugar

½ plus ⅛ teaspoon baking powder

½ plus ⅛ teaspoon salt

1⅜ cups buttermilk

"Cast-iron bread baking was a totally new concept to me when we started," Lauren Crabbe admitted before recounting an anecdote that I found consoling after taking my first stab at these *farls* (or "fourths" in Middle English). She and her Belfast-born husband, Michael McCrory, opened Andytown Coffee Roasters in San Francisco, where she makes his grandmother's quartered bread on the stovetop. In the early stages, Lauren ran into an older Irish neighbor and told him her soda-related troubles. He advised: "Don't beat yourself up over it—it took my wife thirty-five years to get hers right!"

Luckily, there are a lot of good loaves on the way to right. Even my not-so-perfect specimens were a joy to eat, especially when I added a tablespoon of caraway seeds. (You could also try dill, fennel, or anise seeds, cracked pepper, or chopped rosemary.) There's something surprisingly satisfying about making your own bread—from start to finish—in a pan on your stove. The dough takes no time at all, not to stir together or to shape. The less you handle it, the better. And then you get to see it bake right in front of you, not through the glass of an oven window. It's almost like magic, and it comes with a bolstering sense of accomplishment.

1   Using a small fine-mesh sieve, evenly dust the surface of a 10-inch cast-iron skillet with 1 tablespoon of the flour—you should still be able to see some of the pan underneath the layer of white. Preheat the pan over low heat, gradually raising it to medium-low. The skillet should get hot, but not so hot that it burns the flour. Adjust the temperature as necessary.

2   Using a sifter or fine-mesh sieve, sift together the remaining 2½ cups flour, the baking soda, sugar, baking powder, and salt into a large bowl and stir with a whisk to combine. Make a well in the center of the dry ingredients. Pour the buttermilk into the well in a slow, steady stream, stirring with a wooden spoon to combine as you add the liquid. The texture should be wet and sticky. You may not need to use all the buttermilk (start with 1 cup); alternately, if the dough is too dry, add more of the liquid, 1 tablespoon at a time, stirring to incorporate.

(RECIPE CONTINUES)

3 Transfer the dough to a heavily floured surface. With floured hands, quickly and gently form the dough into a loose ball and then knead it into a disc about 8 inches in diameter, taking care not to overwork the dough. Cut a cross into the surface of the dough, creating four equal quarters. The dough will expand and rejoin at the cuts, but clear dividing lines should remain.

4 Make sure the dough is generously floured; otherwise, the bread will stick to the pan. Carefully place the dough in the hot skillet, patting it down so it fills the pan to its edges. It should only be about ½ inch high at this point. Cook the dough for 2 minutes, then raise the heat to medium and cook for 10 to 12 minutes, until it grows to reach just over 2 inches high, its top is dry, and it releases when you shake the pan. Monitor your skillet to avoid burning; you can occasionally rotate the pan, off-center, around the flame to prevent charred spots. If the sides stick, use a butter knife to free them before shaking the bread loose.

5 Use a spatula (or the Upside-Down Plate Trick—see page 56) to flip the dough. If there's evidence of burning flour on the skillet, dust it with a bit more flour to cover the charring patches before returning the dough, flipped, to the pan. Cook on the second side for about 12 minutes, occasionally rotating the pan and the bread itself, until tapping the dough produces a hollow sound. If you see or smell any evidence of burning, reduce the heat immediately, as necessary (though a small bit of char adds flavor). When it's done, the bread will have an airy, fluffy interior. No wet dough should be visible. Cooking time will vary based on weather and pan heat; if you are unsure if your bread is ready, tear it across the pre-cut lines to check it.

6 Remove the finished bread from the pan, swaddle it in a kitchen towel to trap moisture and soften the crust, and let it cool on a wire rack for at least 1 hour.

> **NOTE** Unbleached all-purpose flour will work just as well here; you may need to add a bit more buttermilk to get the right dough consistency.

Loafing Around

To help you master skillet loaves in less than thirty-five years, here are a few things to keep in mind as you find your stovetop groove:

- You're going to need a lot of bench flour, and you shouldn't start second-guessing yourself when you use it. Lauren Crabbe suggests dusting your skillet with flour as much as you would dust brownies with confectioners' sugar.
- It's better if the dough fills the pan all the way to the sides. It won't stick, because of all the flour you're using. Pushing the uncooked loaf all the way out there prevents you from ending up with doughy edges; no one wants those.
- If you are less practiced or dealing with a finicky gas burner, rotate the pan around the flame, slightly off-center. Moving the pan around the flame will allow you to control the distribution of heat. Once you've flipped the loaf to its second side, rotate the bread itself. And if you're more concerned with uneven cooking or burning than you are with doughy edges (as above), then by all means do not pack the loaf tightly into the pan; leave enough space between the dough and the skillet's rim to be able to move the bread itself while the first side is cooking.
- This recipe has a built-in bonus: the layer of flour in your skillet will reveal your pan's hot spots. Even before you put the dough in the pan, the preheating process will have begun to toast the flour, and you can see which—if any—patches are getting browner than the rest.
- When you flip the half-baked bread over, you'll have an even clearer sense of your skillet's trouble areas. Darkening may be more extreme, and if you're a cast-iron-baking beginner, you may end up with a few burnt flour circles. Worse things have happened. The more you get to know your pan, and to make stovetop breads on it, the easier it will be to maneuver your way to evenly cooked loaves.

NUTMEG-SPICED OATMEAL BREAD

makes 1 loaf

½ cup plus 1 tablespoon
  unbleached all-purpose flour,
  plus more for dusting
1¼ cups whole-wheat flour
1 teaspoon baking soda
⅜ teaspoon baking powder

½ plus ⅛ teaspoon salt
⅜ teaspoon freshly grated
  nutmeg, or ½ teaspoon ground
2 teaspoons brown sugar
2 rounded tablespoons steel-cut
  oats, regular or quick-cooking

¾ cup old-fashioned rolled oats
½ cup raisins
1 cup buttermilk, plus more as
  needed

A few years ago, my mother and I decided to continue our tradition of taking long-weekend bonding trips together and went to Portland, Maine, in the fall. Our first stop was Standard Baking Company, where we tried a promising oatmeal raisin cookie. What I especially appreciated about their version was that, instead of having cinnamon—the expected spice—in its dough, it featured nutmeg, which gave it a sharper, more complex, and savory appeal.

I've used the recipe for farls (page 38) as the foundation for a bread that marries oatmeal and raisins—common Irish soda bread ingredients—with nutmeg, same as that cookie. I brought in two types of oats—rolled and steel-cut—a trick borrowed from Martha Rose Shulman, which makes a more textured loaf. Because it's also made with whole-wheat flour, this flat, crusty round has a wonderfully nutty flavor. Its popcornlike aroma gets me every time I set one on the stove.

1 Using a small fine-mesh sieve, evenly dust the surface of a 10-inch cast-iron skillet with 1 tablespoon of the all-purpose flour—you should still be able to see some of the pan underneath the layer of white. Preheat the pan over low heat, gradually raising it to medium-low. The skillet should get hot, but not so hot that it burns the flour. Adjust the temperature as necessary.

2 Using a sifter or fine-mesh sieve, sift together the remaining ½ cup all-purpose flour, the whole-wheat flour, baking soda, baking powder, and the ½ teaspoon salt into a large bowl and stir with a whisk to combine. Add the nutmeg, brown sugar, and steel-cut oats, then whisk everything together again, breaking up any clumps of brown sugar. Add the rolled oats and stir with a wooden spoon to incorporate. Add the raisins and stir again to coat them with the flour.

3   Make a well in the center of the dry ingredients. Pour the buttermilk into the well in a slow, steady stream, stirring with a wooden spoon to combine as you add the liquid. The texture should be wet and sticky. You may not need to use all the buttermilk (start with ¾ cup); alternately, if the dough is too dry, add more of the liquid, 1 tablespoon at a time, stirring to incorporate.

4   Transfer the dough to a heavily floured surface. With floured hands, quickly and gently form the dough into a loose ball and then knead it into a round about 8 inches in diameter, taking care not to overwork the dough.

5   Cut a cross into the surface in the center of the dough and make sure it is generously floured; otherwise, the bread will stick to the skillet. Carefully place the dough in the skillet, patting it down so it fills the pan to its edges. It should only be about ½ inch high at this point. Cook the dough for 2 minutes, then raise the heat to medium and cook for about 10 minutes, until it has risen at least 1 inch, its top is dry, and it releases when you shake the pan. Monitor your skillet to avoid burning; you can occasionally rotate the pan, off-center, around the flame to prevent charred spots. If the sides stick, use a butter knife to free them before shaking the bread loose.

6   Use a spatula (or the Upside-Down Plate Trick—see page 56) to flip the dough. If there's evidence of burning flour on the skillet, dust it with a bit more flour to cover the charring patches before returning the dough, flipped, to the pan. Cook on the second side for 10 to 12 minutes, occasionally rotating the pan and the bread itself, until tapping the dough produces a hollow sound. If you see or smell any evidence of burning, reduce the heat immediately, as necessary (though a small bit of char adds flavor). When it's done, the bread will have an airy, fluffy interior. No wet dough should be visible. Cooking time will vary based on weather and pan heat; if you are unsure if your bread is ready, tear it across the pre-cut lines to check it.

7   Remove the finished bread from the pan, swaddle it in a kitchen towel to trap moisture and soften the crust, and let it cool on a wire rack for at least 1 hour.

FRY BREAD

makes 12 to 16 breads

4¼ cups unbleached all-purpose
flour, plus more for dusting

1 teaspoon salt, plus more for
sprinkling

1 teaspoon baking powder

2 tablespoons milk

1¾ cups warm water

1½ cups lard

1½ cups coconut oil

Rocky Yazzie, founder of a fry bread pop-up in San Francisco, was born into the Diné (more commonly known as Navajo) tribe in New Mexico, where he grew up making this hot, bubbled bread with his grandmother. It was the result, he explains, of an 1883 congressional act that relegated Native American tribes to their respective reservations and rationed their provisions. Fry bread provided an economical way to stretch the small quantity of flour each family was given. Like so much of cuisine born out of poverty, there's nothing skimpy or insufficient about these puffy, light, crispy rounds.

Frying bread is a lot easier than I expected. As Rocky taught me, the dough should be so thin, you can nearly see through it. He prefers lard or coconut oil for frying. Both add flavor—the first will give you something funky; the second, something nutty and mildly sweet. I decided to blend the two and found that they balance each other beautifully. The fat has to be deep enough to allow the dough to float, and hot enough to cook the bread in just a few seconds. You might be surprised to learn—I was—that there's no need for a thermometer; you can tell the fat's ready just by looking at it.

1 In a large bowl, whisk together the flour, 1 teaspoon of the salt, and the baking powder. Add the milk, then, gradually, the warm water, using your hand to work the liquid into the dry ingredients to form a solid ball of dough free of lumps. As it begins to come together in the bowl, use a loose kneading motion to continue to incorporate the water into the flour. Do not overwork the dough. It should be tacky, but not wet. You may not need all the water, or you may need to add a bit more. If there's too much, add more flour, up to a tablespoon at a time, and quickly knead it into the dough until the desired consistency is reached.

2 Cover the dough with a damp kitchen towel and let it rest for 1 hour. It will continue to absorb liquid, and its surface will smooth out.

3 Turn the dough out onto a floured work surface and, using a bench scraper or knife, divide it into 12 to 16 equal-size portions. Holding it in your hands, roll each one into a ball about 2 inches in diameter. Place the

(RECIPE CONTINUES)

balls on a floured cutting board or Silpat and cover them with a damp kitchen towel for 15 minutes.

4   In a 10-inch cast-iron skillet, heat 1 cup each of the lard and coconut oil (enough to fill the pan one-quarter to one-third full), gradually increasing the heat from medium-low to high. When you see the melted fat begin to ripple in rings after about 20 minutes, you're ready to fry. (Another good indicator is a steady, rapid flow of tiny bubbles; if you stick a chopstick into the fat, those same bubbles should immediately rise up around it.)

5   When the frying fat seems close to ready, working one at a time and keeping the others covered, place one of the dough balls on a well-floured work surface and, using a well-floured rolling pin, roll it into a very thin, flat round, 6 to 7 inches wide. It should be so thin that you can almost see through it when it goes into the skillet. Shake off any excess flour, then gently drop it—away from you—into the hot fat. The dough should float up and begin to bubble and puff up immediately. Use a chopstick to make a small (¼-inch) hole in the dough to keep the puffing under control.

6   After 30 seconds to 1 minute, when the underside of the bread is golden, use tongs to flip it over. If it's not quite ready, wait another 30 seconds to 1 minute to flip it. The second side should take about the same amount of time to cook. Once both sides are crisped and golden, use tongs to lift the finished bread out of the skillet. Gently tap the bread against the side of the pan to remove any excess oil and place it on a plate lined with paper towels. Sprinkle the bread with salt and keep it warm in the warming drawer of your oven or in the oven with the temperature below 200°F.

7   Repeat the process with the remaining balls of dough, making sure the fat is hot enough before adding the dough to the skillet. If the oil seems too hot, reduce the heat to medium-high; if it seems too low, raise it back to high. The dough will lower the temperature of the fat and absorb some of it, so check the amount of fat, too. If the center of the bread looks pale and isn't darkening like the rest of the dough, it means there's not enough fat in the pan. Adding a tablespoon of either lard or coconut oil to the skillet after each frying should keep it level, but you may need to add more. Use the moments between removing one finished fried bread and bringing the fat back to the right temperature to roll out the next ball of dough.

8   Eat the fry bread while it's hot. Trickle honey and shake confectioners' sugar over it, or pile it with pinto or black beans, onions, tomatoes, and cilantro.

GREEN PEA PANISSE

makes about 40 batons

3 teaspoons olive oil, plus more
for frying
2½ teaspoons kosher salt,
plus more to taste and for
sprinkling

2¼ cups green pea flour
2 teaspoons sugar
Zest of ½ lemon and/or a
squeeze of lemon, for serving
(optional)

Freshly ground black pepper or
crushed red pepper flakes, for
serving (optional)

As soon as I discovered green pea flour in one of the crammed aisles at my local spice emporium, Kalustyan's, I knew I would use it to make a *panisse*, a chickpea flour–based cake cut into thick, crispy sticks akin to French fries. Who cares if I'd never made one before, even with the requisite flour? Chickpeas are kind of bland anyway. But green peas? They're naturally sweet and taste incredibly verdant, like spring.

Empowered by a *panisse* post on pastry chef and cookbook author David Lebovitz's blog, I assumed it would be easy enough. I would follow his recipe for the polentalike batter, swapping in the green pea for the chickpea flour. I thought wrong. The first time I attempted the batter, I ended up with what looked like lumpy green pudding. I had forgotten that peas cook a lot faster than garbanzos (they really don't need to be cooked at all). I tried the batter again, trusting my pea-guided intuition. On round two, I got it right, and it took less than half as long as it would have had I been making a traditional *panisse*. Once I sliced it and crisped the sticks up in my skillet, I discovered they tasted better, too.

1 Using a paper towel, lightly grease a 9-inch square cake pan or a similar size pan or baking dish with 1 teaspoon of the olive oil.

2 In a medium saucepan, combine 4 cups water, the remaining 2 teaspoons olive oil, and 1½ teaspoons of the salt. Heat the mixture over medium-high heat until the water is hot, but not boiling—just until the tiny bubbles at the bottom of the pan begin to rapidly rise to the surface. Reduce the heat to medium, dump the green pea flour into the pot, and as the flour combines with the water, whisk the mixture continuously for just a minute or so, until it thickens.

3 Switch to a wooden spoon or heatproof spatula and cook the green mixture, stirring continuously, for 2 to 3 minutes, until the batter is bubbling and thick enough to hold its shape. Stirring should be noticeably more difficult, and you should be able to see the bottom of the pan as you drag the

(RECIPE CONTINUES)

spoon through the mixture. Remove the pan from the heat and, working quickly, stir in the sugar and the remaining 1 teaspoon salt. Taste and add more salt as needed. Immediately remove the pan from the heat.

4   Working quickly, while the batter is hot, use a spatula to scrape it into the prepared pan and smooth the top. Press plastic wrap directly against the surface of the batter to prevent a skin from forming and place the pan in the refrigerator for 1 hour to set. (The batter will keep in the refrigerator for up to 2 days.)

5   When you're ready to fry the panisse, unmold the batter (it will have solidified) onto a cutting board and slice it into batons about 3 inches long, 1 inch wide, and ½ inch thick.

6   Fill a 10-inch cast-iron skillet one-quarter to halfway up the sides with olive oil. Heat the oil over low heat, gradually raising the temperature to medium-high. When the oil begins to shimmer, it's hot enough. (To check if it's ready, add a crumb of the panisse batter to the pan. If the oil sizzles up around the crumb, you can proceed.) Fry the panisse sticks in batches of 5 or 6 at a time so as not to crowd the pan. Cook for 3 minutes, or until the bottoms are golden and crisp. Flip

the panisse sticks with tongs and cook for 3 minutes more, or until the other side is also golden and crisp. The exterior should be crispy-thin, while the interior should resemble that of thick-cut French fries or baked polenta—starchy and soft.

7   Place the finished panisse sticks on a paper towel–lined plate and season them aggressively with more salt (about ¼ teaspoon per batch) and, if you like, lemon zest or a squeeze of lemon (or both) and either freshly ground black pepper or red pepper flakes. Repeat with the remaining batons, adding more oil to the skillet if its level drops, and bringing the oil back up to temperature between batches. If the oil gets too hot, reduce the heat accordingly. Season each batch as it comes out of the pan. Expect to get 7 or 8 fry batches from one recipe's worth of batter.

8   Panisse is best eaten right away. If the sticks get too cool, you can reheat them in the oven at a low temperature, or in your cast-iron skillet with a little oil. If you don't want to eat them all at once, you can set half aside, covered, at room temperature, for Panisse Panzanella with Wilted & Raw Lettuces (page 192).

CRUMPETS

makes about 15

2 cups all-purpose flour

1⅓ cups plus 1 tablespoon bread flour

1 heaping teaspoon kosher salt

2⅜ cups whole milk

1½ teaspoons pomegranate molasses

2¼ teaspoons active dry yeast (one ¼-ounce packet)

¼ teaspoon baking soda

¼ cup plus 1 tablespoon warm water

5 teaspoons unsalted butter, plus more for greasing the rings

I spent a semester abroad in London and adhered to a strict diet of those springy, soft griddle cakes hit with a pat of butter and jam, or crème fraîche and smoked salmon, or honey and cheese. If you could put it on a crumpet, I did. When my pants stopped fitting, I knew I had to cut myself off, which was easy enough to do once I returned to the States, where, because people think English muffins and crumpets are interchangeable, you will only find the former. The instant I thought to have the latter in this cookbook, I worried I might fall off the wagon.

Once again, temptation is nigh. This recipe produces the prerequisite galactic holes and proper texture, inside and out, but it does the crumpets of Merry England one better. Anna Higham, a young British pastry cook, had the brilliant notion to put pomegranate molasses in the batter. It heightens the tart, yeasty flavor characteristic of crumpets and maximizes the caramelization that yields a crispy base and rim for their spongy interior. The crumpets make an excellent foundation for the familiar pile-ons of my undergrad days and for a newer Egg Salad Melt with Roasted Asparagus (page 196).

This recipe calls for three crumpet rings, which are inexpensive and readily available online or at any baking supply shop. You jerry-riggers out there will find ways to repurpose empty tuna cans for the cause, but it's okay—you don't need DIY skills to execute this procedure. It's pretty easy. It's also lots of fun, and it fills your kitchen with a magical yeasty fragrance. As Anna says, "It's such a hopeful smell."

1   Whisk together the flours and salt in a large bowl. Set aside.

2   In a medium saucepan, combine the milk, ⅔ cup water, and the molasses, quickly stirring to combine. Gently warm the mixture over low heat until it reaches 110° to 115°F. Remove the pan from the heat and whisk in the yeast. Let the mixture sit for 5 to 10 minutes to activate the yeast. It should be foamy and smell a little sweet and yeasty.

3   Pour the wet mixture into the bowl with the dry ingredients and, using a wooden spoon or rubber spatula, beat the ingredients together for 5 to 10 minutes. You should have a smooth batter. Scrape down the sides of the bowl and cover it with plastic wrap or a kitchen towel. Set aside until the batter has doubled in volume, 45 minutes to 1 hour.

4   Dissolve the baking soda in the warm water and, using a wooden spoon or rubber spatula, beat it into the batter. Scrape down the sides of the bowl once more and let the batter sit for another hour, until it has doubled in volume.

5   About 10 minutes before the batter is ready, preheat a 10-inch cast-iron skillet on the stovetop, gradually raising the heat from low to medium-low. Meanwhile, butter 3 crumpet rings.

6   Once the batter is ready and the pan is hot, raise the heat to medium and add 1 teaspoon of the butter. Tilt the pan to coat, then blot any excess butter with a paper towel so the skillet is slick.

7   Place the greased rings in the skillet and pour a heaping ⅓ cup batter into each. Cook for about 5 minutes, until holes have started to appear around the outer two-thirds of the crumpets. Reduce the heat to medium-low

and, using a spatula, nudge the crumpet rings clockwise, to shift their places in the pan so they cook evenly. After about 5 minutes more, once the entire surface of each crumpet looks dry, using small tongs, remove each ring, then with your spatula, flip the crumpets over and cook them for up to 4 minutes, to give their top sides some color.

8   Using a spatula, transfer the crumpets to a wire rack to cool. Repeat with the remaining batter. Between each batch, raise the heat to medium, add another teaspoon of butter (blotting the excess as before), and re-grease the crumpet rings.

9   Let the crumpets cool completely before toasting them to eat. To store, put them in a sealed container or wrap them in plastic wrap and refrigerate until you're ready to toast them. They'll keep in the refrigerator for up to 3 days.

> **NOTE** Anna also taught me a trick for measuring a dough's rise: "I marked a line on the outside of the bowl with a Sharpie where I judged double to be so that I knew what I was shooting for." Instead of getting indelible ink on my bowl, I used a small, thin strip of masking tape.

TOASTED BARLEY PITA

makes 12 breads

1¾ cups barley flour

½ cup whole-wheat flour

1¼ cups unbleached all-purpose
  flour, plus more for kneading
  and shaping

1 tablespoon active dry yeast

1½ cups warm water

2 teaspoons kosher salt

1 tablespoon plus 1 teaspoon
  extra-virgin olive oil

1 tablespoon honey (optional)

1½ teaspoons olive oil

When I began doing research on skillet-friendly loaves, I found *The Book of Bread*, one of two cookbooks on that subject that Judith Jones and her husband, Evan, wrote together in the 1980s. It had to be a sign. A few months earlier, I'd met Judith, the legendary editor responsible for introducing the American cooking—and reading—public to Julia Child, Madhur Jaffrey, Lidia Bastianich, and Claudia Roden, among others. At ninety, she was still as eager to stand at her stove as she'd ever been. Sometimes, she confessed, at four p.m., she begins to get so excited about the prospect of making dinner that she can't hold off until a more appropriate hour. Her enthusiasm made me want to cook more. I kept my copy of the Joneses' tome within reach while I was working on many of this chapter's breads and on this one, especially.

It's important to have a reliable pita recipe in your repertoire. The bread can be stuffed with whatever you like—egg salad (page 196) is a favorite of mine. I wanted to maintain its versatility, so instead of going crazy with spices or heavy seasoning, I made a minor, flavor-enhancing alteration and applied some toasted barley flour to the dough. You can tell what it's going to do for the pita as soon as you toast it—the flour starts to emit the most wonderful sweet, nutty aroma; it reminds me of the smell of baking biscuits. Each time I placed an uncooked disc on the hot skillet and watched it puff up like a blowfish, I felt like breaking into applause. In those seconds, I thought of Judith. Maybe, at the same time, she was in her kitchen, clapping with uncontained delight over whatever she'd just made for dinner.

1   Preheat a 10-inch cast-iron skillet on the stovetop, gradually raising the heat from low to medium-low. Add the barley flour to the pan and toast it, stirring continuously with a wooden spoon or spatula, for about 10 minutes, until it begins to smell like baking biscuits and slightly darkens in color. Transfer the toasted flour to a medium bowl to cool. Rinse and dry the pan thoroughly.

2   When the toasted barley flour has cooled, add the whole-wheat and all-purpose flours to the bowl and whisk the flours together.

3   In a large bowl, dissolve the yeast in ½ cup of the warm water. Meanwhile, in a smaller bowl, combine the remaining 1 cup warm water with the salt, 1 tablespoon of the extra-virgin olive oil, and the honey (if using). Once the yeast has completely dissolved and is foaming, stir in the contents of the smaller bowl until everything is well combined. Add the flours and stir until a dough forms.

4   Turn the dough out onto a floured surface and, with floured hands, knead it for about 10 minutes. As you work, add extra flour as needed to yield a firm and elastic dough. Clean out the bowl that held the dough, dry it, and rub it with the remaining 1 teaspoon extra-virgin olive oil, blotting any excess with a paper towel. Place the dough in the bowl, turning it so it's evenly coated with the oil. Cover the bowl with plastic wrap and put it in a warm place for about 90 minutes, until the dough has doubled in volume.

5   Place the dough on a large, lightly floured work surface and roll it into a foot-long log. Using a bench scraper, divide the dough into 12 equal portions. Roll each into a ball about 2 inches in diameter. Use your palms to stretch the dough, and your fingers and thumbs to pull the edges down and into the center, tucking them together with a pinch where they meet at the base of the ball. Set them on a floured baking sheet for 5 minutes, covered with a kitchen towel.

6   Working one at a time, keeping the others covered, flatten a dough ball on your work surface with a floured palm, then roll it out into a thin, 6-inch-wide disc using a floured

rolling pin. Return the disc to the floured baking sheet and repeat with the remaining dough balls. Let the discs rest, covered, for 20 minutes.

7   Ten minutes before you plan to cook the pitas, preheat a 10-inch cast-iron skillet on the stovetop, gradually raising the heat from low to medium-high.

8   Add ½ teaspoon of the olive oil to the hot pan and tilt to coat, blotting any excess oil with a paper towel. Place one of the pita discs on the hot pan and cook it for 15 to 20 seconds, then gently flip it over with a spatula. Cook for about 1 minute, until big bubbles begin to emerge on the dough's surface. Flip the bread again and cook until it puffs up like a balloon. You can facilitate this by applying gentle pressure—either with a towel or, if you've got a light enough touch, with your spatula—to the spaces where bubbles have formed. (You want to nudge air into areas in the dough that are still flat.) The entire cooking process should take about 3 minutes. It should be quick, but gradual. If the dough begins to burn, reduce the heat as necessary. Stack the finished pitas under a kitchen towel to keep them warm and prevent them from drying out.

9   Repeat to cook 3 more pitas, then add ½ teaspoon of the olive oil to the pan. Cook 4 more pitas, add the remaining ½ teaspoon olive oil, and cook the remaining discs. Wrapped in plastic, the pitas will keep in the refrigerator for up to 5 days and can be warmed or toasted before serving.

HOECAKE WITH KIMCHI, SCALLIONS & NORI

serves 4 as a side or 2 for lunch

1 cup yellow cornmeal,
  preferably fine ground
  (see Note)
½ teaspoon salt, plus more to
  taste
2½ teaspoons maple syrup

2 tablespoons lard
1 tablespoon canola oil
⅓ cup packed coarsely chopped
  kimchi
2 tablespoons thinly chopped
  scallions (green parts only)

½ teaspoon sesame seeds,
  toasted (see page 26)
3 or 4 (2½ by 4-inch) sheets
  toasted nori, cut widthwise
  into matchsticks or torn into
  confetti-size bits

A hoecake batter is a sludge formed from cornmeal, salt, boiling water, and lard; when fried in a greased, sizzling-hot pan, it develops a crunchy 14-karat-golden crust. Hoecakes are denser than pancakes and both lighter and crunchier than hot-water cornbread. Once a staple of slaves' diets in the American South, they're still served with collard greens to sop up the cooking liquid—or potlikker—left behind. Nashville pastry chef Lisa Donovan taught me how to make them. I snuck maple syrup into her base and decided to pour it all into my skillet in one go. In texture and flavor, the exterior of this large hoecake has all the perks of cornflakes; plus, its interior offers a soft cushion for my teeth to land on. It needed no improvement. Or so I thought, until I tried adding Korean kimchi— along with some toasted nori—on top. This may sound a little kooky and busy. You're just going to have to trust me and give it a try. And keep this in mind: Flipping a single, large fritter is no easy task. If things get messy, you'll be grateful for those garnishes.

1   Preheat a 10-inch cast-iron skillet on the stovetop, gradually raising the heat from low to medium-high, so it gets very hot. Meanwhile, make the batter: In a small saucepan, bring 1⅓ cups water to a boil over high heat. In a large bowl, combine the cornmeal and salt. Add ⅔ cup of the boiling water to the cornmeal and stir to combine. Continue stirring and slowly add 2 tablespoons more water, 1 tablespoon at a time. Add the maple syrup and stir to combine. The batter should be thin enough to slowly pour but also thick enough to spread with a spatula. If the batter is too thick to pour, add more boiling water as needed, 2 teaspoons at a time, and stir to combine.

2   Melt the lard in the hot skillet, tilting to coat, then remove the pan from the heat and pour off the fat into a small heatproof bowl. Add 1 tablespoon plus 1 teaspoon of the melted lard to the batter and stir to combine. Reserve the remaining melted lard.

(RECIPE CONTINUES)

3   Reheat the skillet over medium-high heat until hot. Add the reserved melted lard and the canola oil to the pan and tilt to coat. Pour the batter into the pan. Quickly spread and even out the batter with a spatula or knife, leaving some room around the edges of the skillet for flipping. As the batter cooks, gently jiggle the pan from time to time to prevent sticking. As the edges start to solidify and toast, gently slide your spatula beneath the hoecake and begin to loosen it from the skillet. As frying proceeds, slide the spatula closer to the center of the pan. Cook for about 8 minutes, until the edges are crisp and nicely browned and the rest of the hoecake looks set. If your hoecake is completely loosened from the base of the skillet and slides when you nudge it with your spatula or gently shake the pan, flipping should be no big deal. If the hoecake seems less amenable, use the Upside-Down Plate Trick (see right).

4   Cook for about 6 minutes more, until the second side is golden brown; the interior of the cake should be soft. Turn off the heat and garnish the hoecake, in the pan, with the kimchi, scallions, sesame seeds, and salt to taste. Top it off with the nori and serve hot.

> **NOTE**   Achieving the right batter consistency is important. The coarser your grain, the more water you will likely need to add to the batter. If you're using a medium grind, for example, you may need to add 2 extra *tablespoons* (as opposed to teaspoons) to the mixture.

The Upside-Down Plate Trick

Why does it seem like getting stuff out of your skillet is harder than cooking anything in it? Maybe because it's a hot, heavy pan and there's potential for your food to stick to it. Here's how I do it:

- Make sure the edges of your baked good are completely detached from the cast iron. If needed, run a butter knife around the interior wall of the pan to loosen them.
- Place a plate the same size as the pan (or even slightly larger) over the skillet and, with pot holders, grab hold of both the plate and the pan handle, and turn the duo upside down so the skillet is on top. The cooked item should drop onto the plate.
- If it won't budge, flip it again so the plate is back on top. Set the plate aside and try gently slipping a spatula under the outer rim of the crust to slightly lift the item from the pan.
- Put the plate back over the skillet and try the trick again.
- The same principle applies if you need to flip a facedown baked good from one plate to another to present the finished product right-side up.
- If you have flipped something to cook its other side and need to return it to the pan, carefully slide the item off the plate and into the skillet on the uncooked side and proceed as directed.

LAZY CHEESE AREPAS WITH SLAW

makes 12

6 tablespoons (¾ stick) unsalted butter, melted, plus 1½ teaspoons for the pan

1 cup frozen or fresh sweet corn kernels, thawed and gently patted dry, if frozen

2 cups masarepa (precooked corn flour for arepas), preferably Harina P.A.N.

1 tablespoon sugar

2 cups warm water

1 pound soft fresh cheese, such as queso blanco or queso fresco, or a combination (2⅔ to 3 packed cups)

⅓ pound aged cow's-milk cheese, such as cotija or Pecorino Romano, grated (about 1⅓ cups)

1 teaspoon salt, plus more to taste

3 tablespoons corn oil

Slaw, for garnish (recipe follows)

Your preferred hot sauce, for serving (optional)

These arepas are based on a recipe for the Colombian-style ones, which are distinguished from their Venezuelan counterparts by their flatter, larger shape and the fact that they can be made with yellow—as opposed to white—corn. This, I learned from Maricel E. Presilla's encyclopedic cookbook *Gran Cocina Latina*, where I discovered *arepas de queso asadas*, or grilled corn and cheese arepas.

When Ms. Presilla makes them at home, she chars them under the broiler. I created a similar effect without a grill or an oven (which is where the "lazy" comes from—and where it stops). For textural contrast, I incorporate seared corn kernels into the batter. Then I work at least two types of cheese into the dough. The cool crunch of the lime-splashed slaw makes the corn-flecked arepas seem even warmer, softer, and gooier by comparison. It's worth the extra effort.

1 Preheat a 10-inch cast-iron skillet on the stovetop, gradually raising the heat from low to medium-high. When the pan is hot, add the 1½ teaspoons butter and let it melt, tilting to coat. Add the corn and cook for about 8 minutes, stirring from time to time to avoid sticking, until both sides are burnt. Transfer the charred corn to a small bowl and set aside to cool.

2 In a large bowl, combine the corn flour and sugar. Gradually add the water, incorporating it into the dry ingredients with your fingers. Work in 3 tablespoons of the melted butter, kneading the mixture to form a soft dough. Knead in the cheeses, 1 cup at a time. If the dough seems too dry, add 1 to 1½ tablespoons more water. Taste for seasoning and, if necessary, add the salt to

(RECIPE CONTINUES)

taste, ¼ teaspoon at a time. Keep kneading the dough until it's supple, smooth, and lump-free. It will feel like a cross between lukewarm mashed potatoes and Play-Doh.

3   When the dough is just about right, quickly and gently knead the corn kernels into it and shape it into a compact sphere, working in any remnants that may have stuck to the base of your bowl. Line the bowl with a piece of plastic wrap. Return the dough to the bowl and cover with a damp kitchen towel. Set aside for at least 15 minutes.

4   Preheat the cast-iron skillet on the stovetop, gradually raising the heat from low to medium-high, so it gets very hot. Meanwhile, shape the dough: Divide it into 12 portions of about ½ cup (or 5 ounces) each and place them under a kitchen towel. Working with one at a time and keeping the others covered, roll one piece of dough into a ball, then flatten it into a circle about 3 inches wide and ½ inch thick. Set the finished disc on a plate and cover with a damp kitchen towel. Repeat with the remaining dough, separating the discs with wax paper and keeping them covered as you work.

5   Combine the remaining 3 tablespoons melted butter and the corn oil in a small bowl. Add 1½ teaspoons of the butter-oil mixture to the hot skillet and tilt the pan to coat. Place 4 of the arepas in the pan. Every couple of minutes, rotate them in place, then after 5 minutes, shift them clockwise in the pan, adding 1½ teaspoons more of the butter-oil mixture to the skillet to prevent burning or sticking. At the 10-minute mark, flip the arepas with a spatula and add another 1½ teaspoons of the butter-oil mixture to the pan.

6   Cook the arepas for 8 to 9 minutes more, rotating them in place every couple of minutes and shifting them all together, clockwise, after 4 minutes as above, adding another 1½ teaspoons of the butter-oil mixture to the pan. When finished, the exterior of the arepas should be crisp and solid, and the inside should be cooked through with a soft consistency comparable to cheesy grits. Repeat with the remaining arepas, cooking them in batches of 4 at a time.

7   Eat the arepas immediately while they're hot, or keep them warm on a large plate, covered with aluminum foil, while you cook the rest. Top each with a heaping spoonful of slaw, a pinch of salt, and, if you wish, a few drops of your favorite hot sauce.

(RECIPE CONTINUES)

SLAW

makes about 2½ cups

½ cup sliced jicama, cut into ⅛-inch matchsticks

½ cup sliced apple, cut into ⅛-inch matchsticks

½ cup sliced carrot, cut into ⅛-inch matchsticks

½ cup fennel, thinly sliced horizontally, then
   coarsely chopped to resemble cabbage slaw

¼ cup thinly sliced red onion

3 tablespoons fresh lime juice

1 tablespoon cider vinegar

2 teaspoons honey

1 teaspoon chili powder

2 tablespoons extra-virgin olive oil

¼ teaspoon salt

¼ cup coarsely chopped fresh cilantro,
   for serving

1   In a medium bowl, toss the jicama, apple, carrot, fennel, and onion together so all the ingredients are evenly dispersed.

2   In a small bowl, whisk together the lime juice, vinegar, and honey until the honey has dissolved. Add the chili powder and whisk to combine. Slowly stream the olive oil into the bowl and continue to whisk so the dressing emulsifies. Season the dressing with the salt.

3   Add the dressing to the vegetables, using your hands or a spoon to toss or stir to ensure the vegetables are evenly coated. Mix in the cilantro. You can serve the slaw right away, but it will improve if you leave it in the fridge to marinate for a couple of hours.

GALETTE WITH PICKLISH PLUMS

serves 2 for lunch or 4 for brunch with an assortment of dishes

GINGER-ROASTED PLUMS

3 plums, pitted and cut into large
    chunks

1 shallot, julienned

1 (3-inch) piece fresh ginger,
    peeled, halved, and julienned

1 tablespoon extra-virgin olive oil

3 tablespoons honey

⅛ teaspoon salt

2 tablespoons Ginger Pickling
    Brine, for sautéing (recipe
    follows)

WHIPPED GOAT CHEESE

1 cup (8 ounces) chèvre

1½ tablespoons heavy cream

¾ tablespoon extra-virgin
    olive oil

CRUST

8 tablespoons (1 stick) butter

1 large egg

5½ teaspoons cold water

½ cup buckwheat flour

5½ teaspoons unbleached
    all-purpose flour

5½ teaspoons sugar

½ teaspoon kosher salt

1 teaspoon grapeseed oil

Best-quality fruity extra-virgin
    olive oil, for drizzling

Fine sea salt, for sprinkling

Cracked or coarsely ground pink
    or black peppercorns, for
    sprinkling

I had been researching a galette for my skillet project—more specifically, a traditional Breton-style crepe made with grassy buckwheat flour. I had big plans for this thing—it would be spicy and salty and fruity and made on the stovetop. To get it right, I consulted Devon Gilroy, head of The Corner restaurant at Hotel Tivoli in upstate New York. Devon's technique is as clever as its outcome. Parchment paper lines the bottom of the pan to protect the crust and achieve even browning of the delicate batter. But the real hero here is the fruit topping. Ginger—astringent, warming, and refreshing—gives an acidic, bracing brine a sharp heat. (I wanted to pickle

everything in it; I certainly had enough left over to do so.) When that liquid is combined with the plums, a sliced shallot, and some additional fresh ginger, you get a caramelized, jammy, sweet-and-sour experience like no other. The cooling whipped goat cheese is a breeze to make, which is true of each building block of this stunningly gorgeous, explosively flavored dish, perfect for brunch, lunch, or as part of a fun cheese course. Somehow, it turns a rustic, free-form construction into a work of art that's not too pretty to eat. You'll want to ravish it—I finished the entire galette in one lightning-fast sitting, all by myself.

(RECIPE CONTINUES)

1 **Make the ginger-roasted plums:** Preheat the oven to 450°F. Preheat a 10-inch cast-iron skillet on the stovetop, gradually raising the heat from low to medium-high. In a medium bowl, toss the plums, shallot, julienned ginger, olive oil, 1 tablespoon of the honey, and the salt. When the pan is hot, add the plum mixture. Sauté the fruit for about 7 minutes, stirring frequently with a wooden spoon, until the plums begin to caramelize and soften around the edges.

2 Pour in the 2 tablespoons of the brine, scraping the bottom of the pan with the wooden spoon, and cook the plums for 5 minutes more to allow the juices to thicken and become syrupy. Remove the pan from the heat, add the remaining 2 tablespoons honey, and stir to combine. Transfer the skillet to the oven and roast the plums for about 7 minutes, or until the fruit is somewhat dry and browned around the edges but not burnt. The shallot should be sweet and caramelized, and the plums should be soft around the outside, while retaining some texture toward the center.

3 Transfer the plums and any syrup to a small bowl and set aside. Wipe out the skillet.

4 **Make the whipped goat cheese:** In the bowl of a stand mixer fitted with the paddle, whip the chèvre and cream on medium speed until smooth and aerated. Add the olive oil and continue to mix until incorporated. Transfer the whipped goat cheese to a small bowl and set aside.

5 **Make the crust:** In a small saucepan, melt the butter. Take it off the heat and allow to cool slightly. In a medium bowl, whisk together the egg and cold water. In a separate smaller bowl, combine the flours, sugar, and salt and stir to incorporate. Add the flour mixture to the bowl with the egg and water and, using a wooden spoon, stir until thoroughly combined. Drizzle the melted butter into the batter and whisk until all the ingredients are thoroughly incorporated and the batter is smooth.

6 Set a 10-inch cast-iron skillet on a sheet of parchment paper and trace around the bottom with a pencil. Cut out the circle, following the pencil outline. Repeat to make a second parchment paper round.

7 Drizzle the grapeseed oil into the skillet and tilt to coat. Place one of the parchment paper rounds in the greased skillet. Set the skillet over medium heat for 1 minute. Pour the batter into the heated pan and, using a rubber spatula or the back of a spoon, smooth it into an even layer.

8 Cook the batter for about 1 minute, until small bubbles start to form in the oil around the perimeter of the skillet, then reduce the heat to low. Cook for 18 to 22 minutes more, until the edges of the batter are starting to turn golden, forming tiny bubbles, and the top has begun to set; it should feel powdery to the touch and have a matte finish. Use a spatula to nudge the batter away from the sides of the pan to loosen it and to make sure the bottom is solid and ready to be flipped.

9 Place the other parchment paper round on top of the batter. Using the Upside-Down Plate Trick (see page 56), flip the crust. Gently remove the top parchment. Cook for 5 to 10 minutes more, until the underside is solid and the top is crispy and golden. Using the Upside-Down Plate Trick again, flip the crust out onto a plate and let it cool to room temperature. Once it's cool, remove the remaining parchment.

10 Gently spread the whipped goat cheese over the crust, leaving a ½-inch edge. Spoon the roasted plums over the goat cheese and drizzle as much of their syrup over the galette as you want, along with olive oil, sea salt, and pepper to taste. Serve immediately.

GINGER PICKLING BRINE
makes about 2 cups

2 cups champagne vinegar
1 cup sugar
¼ cup salt
½ teaspoon coriander seed
⅛ teaspoon chili flakes
½ teaspoon black peppercorns
2 thumbs fresh ginger, peeled and julienned

In a medium saucepan, combine all the ingredients with ½ cup water. Stir the mixture to dissolve the sugar and the salt. Bring to a simmer over medium-high heat, then reduce the heat to low and cook for 10 minutes. Remove the pan from the heat and let cool to room temperature. The brine can be refrigerated in an airtight container for up to 2 weeks.

Pickling Advice

After adding the pickling liquid in the Ginger-Roasted Plums preparation, you will have a significant amount left over. Here are a few ideas for using extra brine from Devon and his sous chef, Gemma Kamin-Korn:

- If you're unsure about how much pickling time an item needs, pop a few pieces in a smaller jar and use it as a tester, opening it to check the effectiveness of the liquid and readiness of the ingredients. This allows the rest to remain untouched and sterile.
- For fruits (berries and sliced plums, peaches, or apples), simply pour cold brine over and let them pickle for an hour or two to impart some flavor without overpowering the ingredient.
- For other green vegetables and sulfurous items (broccoli, cauliflower, green beans, radishes, and asparagus), you should also go with cold brine and leave them for at least 3 to 4 days to get very crisp, mild pickles.
- For heartier things, use the liquid while it's still warm (but not hot) and consider parcooking the vegetable. Baby carrots, for example, will take 1 to 2 days treated this way. (Leave them as is and 5 to 7 days is more like it.) Beets, potatoes, and parsnips should be parcooked and pickled for 2 to 3 days.
- Warm, diluted pickling liquid can be used to infuse and rehydrate dried fruits, like apricots and raisins, in dishes that straddle the line between sweet and savory. They would also be an interesting accompaniment on a cheese or charcuterie board.

EASY-BAKE BAKING

Opposite: Carrot-Currant Crostata, page 96

MOM'S CORNBREAD REVISITED

serves 8

8 tablespoons (1 stick) unsalted butter

3 cups finely diced yellow onions (about 3 medium onions)

Scant ¼ teaspoon baking soda

½ teaspoon salt

1 dried bay leaf

1 cup stone-ground cornmeal

1 cup unbleached all-purpose flour

2½ teaspoons baking powder

½ teaspoon freshly ground black pepper

1 cup buttermilk

1 large egg, slightly beaten

½ teaspoon lemon zest

Cornbread was an integral part of our family's corned beef dinner, one of the big Saturday night meals my mother used to cook. In addition to the meat, which was glazed with pineapple, she served brown sugar–baked beans and coleslaw with currants, scallions, and dill. I liked the beef, but it was the sides I'd start dreaming about when she announced the menu during the week. I'd space out in front of my math homework, imagining dredging Mom's cornbread through the gooey beans or the meat's syrupy lacquer. Now, in my own kitchen, with my skillet, I wanted to try something different. I started with caramelized onions, because I love them, and I figured their sweetness would highlight the corn's savory qualities, imparting that—for lack of a better word—*umami* that makes our mouths water.

When researching the best way to caramelize them, I found a *Serious Eats* post by J. Kenji López-Alt that breaks down a faster route. The result is a concentrated golden confit, nearly like a purée, that almost melts into the bread. Adding more butter to the oniony pan served as a way to deglaze the skillet and incorporate those browned bits into the cornbread batter. It was as though, instead of bacon grease, I was cooking with *onion grease*, and it was amazing. You could, of course, add bacon to this cornbread, in lieu of or along with the onions. But like my friend Amy Pennington, urban gardening expert, I'm of the opinion that bacon is "like cleavage." It's obvious. If that's all you got, sure, put some in the pan.

1 Preheat a 10-inch cast-iron skillet on the stovetop, gradually raising the heat from low to medium-high. Place 1 tablespoon of the butter in the pan to melt and as soon as it's sizzling, add the onions, baking soda, ¼ teaspoon of the salt, and the bay leaf. Cook, shaking the pan every couple of minutes, until the onions have released all their liquid and you begin to see brown debris on the bottom or sides of the pan. Add 2 tablespoons water to the pan to deglaze it, giving it a shake and using a wooden spatula or spoon to gently scrape the browned bits off the bottom.

2 Repeat this process up to three more times, until the onions have turned a deep golden brown and most of the residue has dissolved. (If you miss any, don't worry—the butter you add to the pan for the batter will pick up any leftover debris.) All told, cooking the onions should take 25 to 30 minutes.

3 Transfer the onions, with the bay leaf, to a bowl and reduce the heat under the skillet to medium. Add 6 tablespoons of the butter to the pan to melt. Pour the melted butter and any leftover oniony bits into the bowl with the onions and bay leaf. Wipe out the skillet and place it in the oven.

4 Preheat the oven to 400°F. In a large bowl, combine the cornmeal, flour, baking powder, remaining ¼ teaspoon salt, and the pepper. Add the buttermilk, egg, and melted butter from the bowl with the onions and bay leaf and mix everything gently to incorporate. Add the lemon zest to the batter, discarding the bay leaf. Keep the stirring to a minimum; you don't want to overmix the batter.

5 Take the heated skillet out of the oven—with your oven mitts on—and melt the remaining 1 tablespoon butter in it. Pour the batter into the pan, using a rubber spatula to smooth the top. Gently jiggle the skillet—remember those oven mitts—to get rid of any air bubbles and even out the batter.

6 Set the skillet on the middle rack in the oven and bake for 20 to 25 minutes. The cornbread is done when the edges are lightly browned and a cake tester inserted into the center comes out clean. Cut into wedges and serve. Leftover cornbread can be used to make stuffing (page 194).

CHEESY FRITO BREAD WITH PIMIENTOS

serves 8

3½ tablespoons unsalted butter

1 cup yellow cornmeal

½ cup corn flour

⅜ teaspoon salt

1 tablespoon baking powder

½ teaspoon baking soda

½ cup packed Frito crumbs (about 2 cups Frito corn chips pulsed in a food processor)

1 large egg

1½ cups buttermilk

20 shakes of Tabasco sauce (or your preferred hot sauce), or more to taste

1 cup grated extra-sharp cheddar cheese (preferably Tillamook Vintage Extra Sharp White Cheddar)

¼ cup coarsely chopped pimientos

2 tablespoons thinly sliced scallions (white and light green parts)

This cornbread is not in any way traditional, although it is, somehow, an interpretation of a beloved Southern dish: pimiento cheese, the supremely creamy dip made with sharp cheddar, mayo, hot sauce, and the cherry peppers that give the spread its name. It also happens to be made with Fritos corn chips. I probably buried the lede there. The recipe was designed for the skillet, but a vintage corn stick pan is a sweet way to present the bread (just bake them a few minutes less).

1   Preheat the oven to 350°F with a 10-inch cast-iron skillet in it. In a small saucepan, melt 2 tablespoons of the butter over medium-low heat. Once the butter has melted, remove the pan from the heat and set it aside.

2   Sift the cornmeal, corn flour, salt, baking powder, and baking soda into a large bowl. Using a whisk, stir in the Frito crumbs.

3   In a medium bowl, beat together the melted butter and the egg. Stir the buttermilk into the egg and butter mixture to combine. Add the hot sauce (as much as you can stand) and stir again to combine. Fold the wet ingredients into the dry to incorporate completely. Fold in the cheese, pimientos, and scallions.

4   Remove the skillet from the oven and place the remaining 1½ tablespoons butter in it to melt. Once the butter is sizzling, use your spatula to scrape the batter into the pan, smoothing the top and giving the skillet a gentle shake to even it out.

5   Bake the cornbread for 30 minutes, until the edges are brown, the top is golden, and the bread has pulled away from the sides of the pan a little. You can serve it straight from the skillet, or, if you wish, turn it out onto a plate; use a spatula to loosen the cornbread from the pan to avoid any sticking.

SESAME BROWN-BUTTER CORNBREAD

serves 8

6 tablespoons (¾ stick) unsalted
   butter

1 cup stone-ground cornmeal

⅓ cup coconut flour

¼ cup sesame or benne seeds,
   toasted (see page 26)

⅓ cup coconut sugar

2½ teaspoons baking powder

¼ teaspoon baking soda

¾ teaspoon salt

½ cup buttermilk

½ cup vanilla ice cream, melted
   (see Note)

1 large egg, slightly beaten

1 tablespoon coconut oil

Brown butter is what you get when you cook the fat until its water has evaporated and its milk solids have begun to toast, turning a lovely hazelnut hue that reminds me of the top of a crème brulée. Just as that custard, with its hard crust of crisp caramelized sugar, was big in the 1980s (thanks to Sirio Maccioni and his pastry chef Dieter Schorner at the legendary New York City restaurant Le Cirque), thirty years later, brown butter appears to be having a similar moment. People are throwing it into brownies, blondies, cakes, cookies, and, yes, even cornbread. Browning takes everything I love about butter and intensifies it, then tacks on a bonus: a deep, nutty note.

On the matter of sugar in savory cornbread, I side with whichever faction of the divided South is anti: I will have none of it in my batter. But this sweet cornbread isn't like anything you've had before. I still can't quite put my finger on it—its nuttiness is similar to, though less pronounced than, what peanut butter tends to give off when baked into batters. It's a real surprise, this recipe—a pleasant one.

1   Preheat a 10-inch cast-iron skillet on the stovetop, gradually increasing the heat from low to medium. Once the pan is hot, add the butter, tilting to coat. As it melts, it will sizzle and foam. Continue to cook the butter until the foam dissolves and the liquid turns the color of hazelnuts, a rich brown. (Make sure it doesn't burn.) If it's spattering too much, reduce the heat a bit. Pour the brown butter into a small heatproof bowl and set aside to cool. Wipe out the skillet.

2   Preheat the oven to 400°F with the skillet in it. In a large bowl, using a whisk, stir together the cornmeal, coconut flour, sesame seeds, coconut sugar, baking powder, baking soda, and salt.

3   In a medium bowl, whisk together the buttermilk, melted ice cream, and egg to combine. Continue to whisk as you add the brown butter, drizzling it in to incorporate it gradually.

4   Add the wet ingredients to the dry ingredients, whisking to thoroughly incorporate. The batter will seem on the dry side. Don't worry.

5   Take the hot skillet out of the oven and add the coconut oil, tilting to coat. Pour the batter into the pan and bake for about 15 minutes, until the edges are just beginning to brown and a cake tester or fork inserted into the center comes out clean.

6   You can serve it straight from the skillet, or, if you wish, turn it out onto a plate—just use a spatula to loosen the edges and bottom of the cornbread from the pan first, to avoid any sticking. Cut it into 8 wedges. Enjoy it for breakfast, or as an afternoon snack.

NOTE   Whenever possible, I prefer to allow the natural sweetness of fats to shine through in my baked goods. It's why you'll notice vanilla ice cream in this recipe. Make sure you choose the best-quality ice cream you can find—one with a high butterfat content that isn't cloying. It lends moisture and gives you a tender crumb.

ONE-PAN POPOVER

serves 4 to 6 as a snack

¾ cup all-purpose flour

¾ cup kamut flour

1½ teaspoons kosher salt

1 teaspoon freshly ground black
  pepper

½ cup grated Parmesan cheese

2½ tablespoons packed minced
  fresh chives, or more to taste
  (see Note)

½ teaspoon lemon zest (see Note)

1½ cups milk

1½ tablespoons plus ½ teaspoon
  duck fat

3 large eggs

Ricotta Spread (recipe follows),
  for serving

When is a Dutch baby pancake no longer a Dutch baby pancake? When it's a popover. And when is it no longer a popover? When it's a Yorkshire pudding. Though the latter is prepared with beef fat (usually the reserved drippings from a roast), its batter is frighteningly similar to that of a popover: both are made from flour, eggs, and milk—just use melted butter instead of the beef fat, and you're there. Yorkies and popovers call for designated tins that look like muffin pans to produce multiple smaller portions. That's not true of Dutch babies; they're solitary, giant, puffed-up pancakes. After trying to understand what distinguishes each of these souffléed batters from the others, I've decided the differences are negligible enough to render them nearly interchangeable.

This one-pan popover packs as much flavor as possible with chives, lemon zest, Parmesan, and duck fat, which imparts a faintly sweet, subdued gaminess and makes for a more golden exterior and tender interior. As I watched the slow sigh of a rise through my oven window, I saw my creation go from fluffy,

thin-skinned Dutch baby to high, crispy-domed popover—or maybe it's a giant Yorkshire pudding because of its nonvegetarian fat. The ricotta topping turns it into something else altogether. (So don't even think about leaving it out.)

1   In a medium bowl, sift the flours together. Add the salt, pepper, 3 tablespoons of the Parmesan, the chives, and the lemon zest and stir together to combine. Set the mixture aside.

2   In a small saucepan, heat the milk over medium-low heat just until it starts to bubble around the edges of the pan. Make sure it doesn't boil and stir it occasionally to prevent a skin from forming. Remove the pan from the heat immediately, pour the milk into a small bowl, and set it aside.

3   Rinse and dry the saucepan and return it to the stove. Add 1½ tablespoons of the duck fat to melt over medium heat. Once the fat has melted, pour it into a separate small bowl and set it aside.

4   In the bowl of a stand mixer fitted with either the paddle or whisk (or in a bowl with a handheld electric mixer, or by hand with a whisk), beat the eggs on medium speed until they're frothy. Gradually incorporate the warm milk into the eggs. Add the flour mixture, reduce the speed to low, and mix until the ingredients are well incorporated; scrape down the sides of the bowl if necessary. Mix in the melted duck fat. Cover the batter and refrigerate for at least 1 hour or up to 24 hours—the longer, the better.

5   Position the top rack in the middle or lower third of the oven and place a 10-inch cast-iron skillet on it. Preheat the oven to 450°F.

6   When the oven comes to temperature, remove the batter from the refrigerator and whisk it. Take the skillet out of the oven and melt the remaining ½ teaspoon duck fat in it, using a pastry brush to wipe the fat over the bottom and sides of the pan. Pour the batter into the pan and sprinkle the remaining Parmesan over the top.

7   Bake for 20 minutes, then, without opening the oven, reduce the oven temperature to 350°F and bake for 15 minutes more, until the popover is puffed and deeply browned. Serve the popover immediately, in the skillet, or carefully transfer it to a large plate, with the ricotta topping on the side.

> **NOTE**   If you're keen on chives, increase the amount to 5 tablespoons. If you're not a lemon lover, halve the zest or cut it altogether. Keep in mind, though, that those green and yellow flecks of freshness offset the duck fat.

RICOTTA SPREAD
makes 1 cup

1 cup fresh ricotta cheese
1 tablespoon minced fresh chives
1 teaspoon flake salt
Freshly ground black pepper

In a small bowl, stir together all the ingredients to combine. You can prepare this a day or two in advance and refrigerate it, but it's best served the same day it's made.

SOCCANATA WITH LAMB, OLIVES & OREGANO

serves 4

SOCCANATA

1 cup chickpea (garbanzo) flour
(see Notes)

1½ teaspoons salt

1 teaspoon freshly ground black
pepper

1 teaspoon ground sumac

2 tablespoons extra-virgin
olive oil

2 cups shredded zucchini (about
1 large zucchini; see Notes)

LAMB TOPPING (OPTIONAL)

1 teaspoon olive oil

½ large onion, minced

½ pound ground lamb
(not too lean)

½ teaspoon salt

½ teaspoon ground sumac

½ teaspoon ground cumin

¼ teaspoon ground cinnamon

1½ teaspoons coarsely chopped
fresh oregano leaves

2 heaping tablespoons coarsely
chopped green olives
(picholine, preferably)

1 teaspoon coarsely chopped
fresh oregano leaves

1 tablespoon plus 1 teaspoon
olive oil, plus more as needed

Greek yogurt, for serving

On the Côte d'Azur of France, they call it *socca;* across the border in Italy, it's *farinata*. Both words refer to the same thing: a chickpea griddle cake that is often described as a crepe, but has a stronger presence. The foundation for an intensely flavorful meal, this one is so much more than a *socca*, or *farinata*, which is why I lovingly refer to it as a combination of the two words: it is my *soccanata*. Mark Bittman's recipe for *socca* gave me the idea to pan-roast the zucchini I use to bolster the sumac-infused batter. I build on that with a topping of heavily—and heavenly—spiced ground lamb, prepared in the same cast-iron skillet as the rest. When the garbanzo base emerges from the oven, it is good enough to eat on its own, split into hot shards with your hands—or, even better, with the meat and a garnish of cooling, creamy Greek yogurt spooned on top.

1   Prepare the soccanata: In a medium bowl, stir together the chickpea flour, 1 teaspoon of the salt, the pepper, and sumac to combine. Pour in 1 cup lukewarm water and whisk until the batter is smooth, without any lumps. (If you're having a hard time getting a smooth consistency, use an immersion blender.) Stir in the extra-virgin olive oil, cover, and let the batter rest at room temperature for at least 30 minutes and up to 12 hours, or refrigerate overnight, so the flour can fully absorb the water. (The batter will keep in the refrigerator for up to 3 days.)

2   Preheat the oven to 450°F. (If you're not making the lamb topping, then place the skillet in the oven to preheat.)

(RECIPE CONTINUES)

3   In a medium bowl, toss the zucchini with the remaining ½ teaspoon salt and let it sit for 5 minutes. Place the zucchini in a sieve set over a bowl and push it against the sieve to squeeze out the water. Alternatively, you can place the zucchini in a kitchen towel or cheesecloth and wring the liquid out. Put the zucchini in a dry bowl; set it aside.

4   **Make the topping (if using):** Preheat a 10-inch cast-iron skillet on the stovetop, gradually raising the heat from low to medium-high. When the pan is hot, add the olive oil and tilt to coat. Once the oil is hot, add the onion and sauté, stirring frequently with a wooden spoon, for about 5 minutes, until it begins to soften and turn translucent.

5   Add the lamb to the skillet, using the spoon or a spatula to break up the meat. Add the salt, sumac, cumin, and cinnamon and stir to combine. Stir in the oregano and olives. Cook, stirring continuously, for about 10 minutes, until the meat is cooked through. Transfer the mixture to a bowl and cover with aluminum foil to keep warm. Drain any remaining lamb fat from the pan, reserving 1 tablespoon. Do not clean the skillet.

6   Return the reserved 1 tablespoon fat to the hot skillet and tilt to coat. (If you don't have enough fat, use olive oil to make up the difference. If your skillet is not hot enough—it should sizzle—put it in the oven for 5 minutes to heat up before adding the oil.) If you're not making the lamb, take the skillet out of the oven and add 1 tablespoon of the olive oil. Add the drained zucchini to the skillet and put it in the oven. Roast the zucchini for 8 to 10 minutes, stirring it once or twice, until it's just starting to brown.

7   **Finish the soccanata:** Take the skillet out of the oven and stir the oregano into the zucchini. Add the zucchini to the batter and whisk to combine. Quickly brush the surface of the hot skillet with 1 teaspoon of the olive oil. Immediately pour the batter into the pan and return the pan to the oven. Bake the soccanata for 10 to 12 minutes, until the center is firm and springy and the edges are set. Remove the skillet from the oven and turn on the broiler. Using a pastry brush or the back of a spoon, swipe the top of the soccanata with the remaining 1 tablespoon olive oil. Return it to the oven, a few inches beneath the broiler, and broil for 3 minutes, until the surface is lightly freckled with brown spots.

8   Serve the soccanata hot, straight from the skillet, or, if you want to remove it, wait a minute or two before gently loosening the edges with a spatula and flipping it out onto a serving plate. Top it with the lamb mixture, if using. Place a dollop of Greek yogurt in the center or serve it in a bowl on the side.

NOTES

- Chickpea flour makes this *socca* safe for anyone avoiding gluten.

- I like to shred zucchini in a food processor with the shredding blade because it yields a slightly coarser texture, but you can also use a box grater if you'd rather.

SWIRL BREAD WITH LEEKS, TAHINI & DILL

makes 1 loaf

DOUGH

2 teaspoons active dry yeast

1 tablespoon maple syrup (or honey; see Note)

1 cup warm water (110° to 115°F)

3 cups whole-wheat flour, plus more for dusting

1 teaspoon salt

1 tablespoon olive oil

FILLING

1½ teaspoons olive oil

2½ cups thinly sliced leeks (about 2 large leeks), well rinsed in a colander under cold water and dried

2 tablespoons vermouth

¾ teaspoon salt

¼ teaspoon freshly ground black pepper

½ cup tahini

1 tablespoon maple syrup (or honey; see Note)

2 tablespoons sesame seeds, toasted (see page 26)

2 tablespoons chopped fresh dill

2 tablespoons plus 1 teaspoon olive oil

1½ tablespoons sesame seeds, for sprinkling

Usually the label "whole wheat" or "vegan" is enough to deter me from flagging a recipe, but one for Whole Wheat Tahini Chocolate Bread that I found on a blog called *Dreamy Leaf* by a chef named Maya Sozer looked so pretty and delicious. I was swayed by the bread's swirled shape and the inclusion of tahini. This savory riff on the sweet original upholds the wholesome end of the bargain. When you start to think about all those teasing Pillsbury commercials with families gathered around the table grabbing hot dinner rolls off a plate and melting pats of butter on them, you might feel a pang of pity for your vegan friends. They deserve a freshly baked, tempting bread of their own to tear into. And if it's one that those of us who aren't vegans can enjoy just as much, then all the better.

1   **Start the dough:** In a small bowl, dissolve the yeast and maple syrup in the warm water, gently stirring to incorporate. Set aside for about 5 minutes, until the yeast has dissolved and begun to foam.

2   In a large bowl, stir together the flour and salt with a wooden spoon. Add the yeast mixture and olive oil and stir just until the dough begins to come together. Start kneading the dough in the bowl, using your hand to incorporate any extra liquid or flour. If there's not enough water, slowly add a bit more—a teaspoon or two at a time, up to ¼ cup—as needed. The dough should be soft and supple, not sticky or wet. After about 5 minutes of kneading, cover the bowl and let the dough rest for an hour, until it has doubled in size.

(RECIPE CONTINUES)

3   **Meanwhile, make the filling:** Preheat a 10-inch cast-iron skillet on the stovetop, gradually raising the heat from low to medium-high. Once the pan is hot, add the olive oil and tilt to coat. Add the leeks and sauté for about 8 minutes, until they are soft and just begin to brown. Deglaze the pan with the vermouth. When the liquid has cooked off, remove the pan from the heat and season the leeks with ¼ teaspoon of the salt and the pepper.

4   Transfer the leeks to a medium bowl. Preheat the oven to 350°F with a skillet in it. Add the tahini, maple syrup, and leeks and use a rubber spatula to combine. Incorporate the sesame seeds and the dill into the mixture. Taste and season with the remaining ½ teaspoon salt. Set the filling aside.

5   **Finish the dough:** Place the dough on a well-floured work surface and, using a floured rolling pin, flatten and spread the dough as thin and wide as you can (mine was approximately 17 by 14 inches). Using a rubber spatula, spread the leek filling over the surface of the dough and roll it into a tight log. Using a sharp knife, slice the log in half down the middle lengthwise so you have two snakelike ropes of dough. Twist each of the dough snakes a few times to elongate and thin them somewhat to allow you to fit them into the skillet properly.

6   Take the hot pan out of the oven and add 1 teaspoon of the olive oil to coat. Spiral the dough ropes into the skillet, starting with one in the center of the pan, and then wrapping the second around it to fill the pan (see photographs on page 154). Brush the top of the spiraled dough with the remaining 2 tablespoons olive oil and sprinkle the untoasted sesame seeds over the top. Bake for about 45 minutes, until the top is golden brown.

7   Like any freshly baked loaf, this bread is good straight out of the oven. Some might say that, when left covered at room temperature, it's even better the next day. Serve it in the skillet or transfer it to a large plate; leave it intact so you don't lose the dramatic presentation. Tear into it, or neatly slice a wedge.

NOTE I first made this bread with honey, not realizing it isn't vegan. (You live, you learn.) It's delicious with either sweetener, so if you're not vegan and you don't have maple syrup, honey is just as good.

BROCCOLI CAKE

serves 4 to 6

4 cups packed broccoli florets with 1 to 1½ inches of their stalks attached

4 teaspoons olive oil

¼ teaspoon coarse salt

1 cup finely diced onion (about 1 medium)

3 tablespoons thinly sliced scallions (white and light green parts)

¾ teaspoon fine salt

¼ teaspoon freshly ground black pepper

1 cup all-purpose flour

1½ teaspoons baking powder

¼ teaspoon ground turmeric

½ teaspoon smoked paprika

½ teaspoon sweet paprika

1 teaspoon toasted cumin seeds (see page 26)

5 large eggs

3 tablespoons sour cream

1½ packed cups grated aged Gouda

¼ cup pumpkin seeds, toasted (see page 26)

½ tablespoon unsalted butter

While flipping through *Plenty More*, Yotam Ottolenghi's second tome on vegetable cookery, I spied a photo of a stunning cauliflower cake. Its top was golden, with purple onion rings set into it like pressed flowers, and its edges were coated in white sesame and black nigella seeds. It reminded me of a dish my mother used to make called Broccoli Mold. I know, that sounds positively dreadful. You're thinking aspic, or maybe green, fuzzy, old-food mold. Stop it immediately! Instead, picture fresh, tender florets with scallions, sour cream, Swiss cheese, nutmeg, and almonds. Then try to imagine what would happen if you brought those items to Ottolenghi's creation. That's what I've done, with some adjustments.

To make it more of a cake and less of a frittata, I use the same amount of flour as Yotam does, but two fewer eggs. The result is something that, texturally, reminds me of a mildly bready Spanish tortilla, and like a tortilla, this broccoli thingamajig is great warm or at room temperature. I couldn't resist tasting it when it came out of the oven, though. I had invited my mother over to test it out with me. As usual, she distracted me with her mom talk, thinking the cooking part was just an excuse to gossip. Fortunately, the recipe is so easy, you can't really mess it up, even if Chatty Cathy invades your kitchen. Of course, had it not been for Mom, I wouldn't have come up with this savory vegetable cake at all.

1 Preheat the oven to 425°F. Split the broccoli florets lengthwise so that each is about ⅛ inch thick, using your knife to slice through the stems, then pulling the florets apart. Place the split broccoli spears on a baking sheet big enough that you can spread them out in one layer. Sprinkle 2 teaspoons of the oil and the coarse salt over the florets and toss to evenly coat. Roast for about 15 minutes, until the florets are just beginning to brown. Transfer the roasted broccoli to a small bowl and set it aside to cool.

2 Meanwhile, preheat a 10-inch cast-iron skillet on the stovetop, gradually raising the heat from low to medium-high. When the pan is hot, add the remaining 2 teaspoons oil and tilt to coat. Give the oil a few seconds to heat up, then add the onion and scallions and sauté, stirring frequently with a wooden spoon or spatula, for 3 to 5 minutes, until they soften and begin to turn translucent. Transfer the onion and scallions to a large bowl, season with ¼ teaspoon of the fine salt and the pepper, and set aside to cool. Rinse and dry the skillet.

3 Preheat the oven to 400°F with the skillet in it.

4 Sift the flour, baking powder, the remaining ½ teaspoon fine salt, the turmeric, and smoked and sweet paprikas into a medium bowl. Add the toasted cumin seeds and toss to combine.

5 Add the eggs to the bowl with the onion-scallion mixture and whisk vigorously to combine. Add the dry ingredients, whisking to form a thick batter. Whisk in the sour cream. Switch to a wooden spoon and stir in the Gouda, followed by the pumpkin seeds and, finally, the roasted broccoli. Make sure the ingredients are thoroughly incorporated, being careful not to break the broccoli florets as you stir.

6 Remove the hot skillet from the oven and add the butter to melt, brushing it over the bottom and sides of the pan. Using a rubber spatula, scrape the batter into the skillet, spreading it to fill the pan and smoothing the top. Bake for about 20 minutes, until the top is golden brown, the center has set, and a cake tester inserted into the center comes out clean. Wait 5 minutes, then flip it out so it's right-side up using the Upside-Down Plate Trick (see page 56). Let it cool slightly, at least 10 to 15 minutes, before serving; it's best eaten warm or at room temperature.

DATE, ONION & FONTINA SCONES

makes 8 scones

1 tablespoon plus 1 teaspoon unsalted butter, per batch

3 cups finely diced yellow onions (about 3 medium onions)

¾ teaspoon plus ⅛ teaspoon baking soda

1¼ teaspoons salt

1 teaspoon packed orange zest

1¾ cups unbleached all-purpose flour, plus more for dusting

1¾ cups barley flour

1 tablespoon baking powder

9½ tablespoons unsalted butter, cut into cubes and chilled

1½ cups loosely packed coarsely grated Fontina cheese

½ cup packed finely grated Parmesan

2 tablespoons plus 1 teaspoon date syrup

1¼ cups heavy cream

1 cup chopped pitted Medjool dates

One of the things that separate West Coast pastry chef William Werner's work from the rest of the pack is its aesthetic style. It's sorta like rock 'n' roll, with flowers. At his Craftsman and Wolves shops, there's always something rebellious at play; visually arresting, traditional baked goods and breads showcase unusual seasonal ingredients and often blur the line between savory and sweet. In the fall, I love his apple-Gruyère scone, topped with a large crown of melted cheese from beneath which thin slices of baked apples poke out.

Fruit and cheese are a classic pairing. You get sweet and salty in one perfectly harmonized bite. To create my own combo, I took William's recipe apart and put it back together, in a remarkably easy case of substitution. One day, when I'm feeling more The Melvins than Cat Power, I'm going to send him *my* recipe, so he can try it and tell me what he thinks. For now, I'm content to sit at my desk with a cup of tea, one of these scones, and a pitcher full of peonies.

1   Preheat a 10-inch cast-iron skillet on the stovetop, gradually increasing the heat from low to medium-high. Once the pan is hot, add 1 tablespoon of the butter. As soon as it's melted and sizzling, add the onions, ¼ teaspoon of the baking soda, and ¼ teaspoon of the salt. Cook the onions, shaking the pan every couple of minutes, until they've released all their liquid and you begin to see brown debris on the bottom or sides of the skillet.

2   Add 2 tablespoons of water to deglaze the pan, giving it a shake and using a wooden spatula or spoon to gently scrape the brown bits off the bottom. Repeat the deglazing process up to three more times, until the onions have turned a deep golden. All told, cooking the onions should take 25 to 30 minutes. Place them in a small bowl with the orange zest, stir to combine, and set aside. Rinse and wipe out the pan.

3   Sift the remaining ½ plus ⅛ teaspoon baking soda, remaining 1 teaspoon salt, the flours, and the baking powder together into the bowl of a stand mixer. Add the 9½ tablespoons cubed and chilled butter and toss to coat with the flour mixture. Cover and refrigerate for 25 minutes.

4   Preheat the oven to 375°F with the skillet in it.

5   In a small bowl, toss ¾ cup of the Fontina and the Parmesan together and set aside. In a medium bowl, whisk together the caramelized onions, date syrup, and cream. Affix the stand mixer bowl with the butter and dry ingredients to the mixer and fit it with the paddle. Mix on low speed for about 2 minutes, until the butter breaks down into pea-size pieces. Add the onion-cream mixture and mix for a few seconds until just incorporated, then add the dates, followed by the remaining ¾ cup Fontina. It should take only a few seconds for everything to combine; don't overmix the dough.

6   Turn the dough out onto a lightly floured work surface and pat it into a 1½-inch-thick block. Using a bench scraper, slice it into four 3½-inch squares and then cut each square on the diagonal, forming two triangles per square. Sprinkle the triangles with the Fontina-Parmesan mixture.

7   Remove the hot skillet from the oven, place 1 teaspoon butter in it to melt, and tilt (or brush) to coat. Place 3 or 4 dough triangles in the pan and bake for 25 to 30 minutes, until they're golden brown and cooked through. While those are baking, place the remaining triangles on a plate lined with wax paper, cover them with plastic wrap, and place them in the refrigerator. Leave the finished scones in the skillet for 10 minutes before transferring them to a plate to finish cooling. When you are ready to bake the rest, remove them from the refrigerator and follow the above process, melting 1 teaspoon of butter in the skillet before adding the triangles and putting them in the oven. Serve the scones at room temperature.

8   If you prefer to bake the remaining dough triangles later, layer them between wax paper in an airtight container and store them in the refrigerator overnight or in the freezer for up to 1 month. You don't need to defrost them before baking them, but you should keep them in the oven a couple of minutes longer. You can sprinkle them with the Fontina-Parmesan mixture before storing them, or sprinkle the triangles with the cheese right before you bake them. To bake, follow the directions above.

> **NOTE**   William makes his scones in a stand mixer, which is how I did it, to show proper respect. You could do it by hand, or in a food processor, if you prefer.

SPICED BUTTERNUT SQUASH BISCUITS

makes 18 biscuits

½ medium butternut squash, halved lengthwise and seeded (see Notes)

1½ teaspoons olive oil

¼ teaspoon kosher salt

2 teaspoons honey

2 teaspoons Sriracha

½ teaspoon ground ginger

1¼ plus ⅛ teaspoons fine salt

3¼ cups bleached all-purpose flour (preferably White Lily; see Notes), plus more for dusting

2½ teaspoons baking powder

8 tablespoons (1 stick) unsalted butter, cut into ½-inch cubes and chilled, plus ½ tablespoon

⅓ cup whole or low-fat milk

After possibly getting myself permanently banned from the South with my crème fraîche biscuits (page 98), I wanted to create one that followed protocol, technically speaking. In terms of the flaky, pillowy, tender outcome and method for achieving that, I went by the book; two, in fact. Virginia Willis's sweet potato biscuits, from her cookbook, *Basic to Brilliant, Y'all*, are spot-on. Everyone loves them, my dad—the toughest critic—included. I did a variation with another fall regular, butternut squash, which may be less Southern than the tuber, but is a great vehicle for unexpected, sharper flavors. I roasted the squash, then combined it with honey and Thai Sriracha sauce.

Then I turned my attention to food writer Belinda Ellis's "kneading" process. (With all the years she spent studying, teaching, and making biscuits, someone should give her an honorary doctorate!) Rather than a pushing and pulling motion, hers is a series of simple folds and pats—nothing complicated or time-consuming. My biscuits rose so high, I was

almost convinced I had a special gift. A second burst of pride followed when I took a bite and experienced a surprising, unexpected wave of complex sweetness, followed by a sneaky hit of heat. The flavors had melded together to create something unique and irresistible. I believe these towering butternut-stained biscuits might just be good enough to get me back into the good graces of my Southern friends.

1 Preheat the oven to 400°F. Coat the flesh and skin of the squash with the olive oil and sprinkle with the kosher salt. Place the squash on a baking sheet, cut-side down, and roast until it's very soft, about 1 hour. Remove the baking sheet from the oven and let the squash cool for at least 20 minutes. Once it's cool, scoop out the flesh, discarding the skin. Place the flesh in a food processor and process until smooth. (The puréed squash will keep in an airtight container in the refrigerator for up to 3 days.)

(RECIPE CONTINUES)

NOTES

- White Lily Flour is extremely light, which means that dough made with it requires less liquid. (If you're using another brand of bleached all-purpose flour, you may end up with slightly drier dough.) If it's too dry, you can add a bit more milk to the dough when it's still in the food processor—1 tablespoon or even a couple of teaspoons at a time, to be safe. Alternatively, if the dough seems a little too wet when you turn it out, dust your work surface with extra flour, adding more, if needed, until you're able to fold and pat the dough.

- To freeze the biscuits, place the unbaked rounds on a parchment paper–lined baking sheet, cover them with plastic wrap, and put them in the freezer. Once they're completely frozen, transfer them to a plastic bag. They'll keep in the freezer for up to 2 months. Take them out while the oven is preheating and bake as directed (they may need an extra minute or two).

2   When you're ready to make the biscuits, preheat the oven to 400°F with a 10-inch cast-iron skillet in it.

3   Place 1 cup of the puréed squash in a medium bowl, reserving the rest for another use (like Roasted Vegetable Cobbler, see page 198). Add the honey and Sriracha to the bowl and stir to combine. Add the ginger and ½ plus ⅛ teaspoon fine salt and stir again.

4   In the food processor, pulse the flour, baking powder, and the remaining ¾ teaspoon of the fine salt a few times to mix them together. Add all but 2 of the cubes of butter, a few at a time, and pulse to combine, until you have what looks like coarse meal.

5   Add the milk to the bowl with the squash purée and whisk until well combined and the mixture is smooth. Add the squash mixture to the food processor, pulsing just until a moist dough has formed. If it's too dry, add more milk, a tablespoon or couple of teaspoons at a time, and pulse to incorporate.

6   Turn the dough out onto a lightly floured work surface, cradling it with lightly floured hands to gently form it into a block, then patting the top to flatten it into a rectangle about ¼ inch thick. Fold the dough in half, give it a pat, then fold it in half again. Lift the dough (use a bench scraper if there's any sticking, and dust the work surface with flour as needed), put it back down, and pat it

again. Repeat the folding and patting a few more times, just until the dough is smooth and no longer sticky.

7   Pat the dough and flatten it to a ¾-inch thickness. Press—without twisting—a 2-inch biscuit cutter straight down into the dough to cut out rounds, getting as many as you can out of the initial rectangle of dough, and place the rounds on a piece of wax paper as you go. Pile the scraps on top of one another in layers and pat them out to form another rectangle; cut as many more rounds from it as you can. Repeat until there is no dough left.

8   Take the hot skillet out of the oven and melt the 2 remaining ½-inch butter cubes in it, tilting the pan to coat. Place half of the cut biscuits in the pan and bake for 10 to 15 minutes, until a cake tester inserted into the center of a biscuit comes out clean. While those are baking, place the remaining half of the cut biscuits—still on the wax paper—on a large plate or tray so they can lie flat, cover them with plastic wrap, and place them in the refrigerator.

9   Remove the skillet from the oven and wait for 5 minutes before transferring the hot biscuits to a wire rack to cool for 10 minutes or so more. Repeat with the remaining cut biscuits, remembering first to place the additional ½ tablespoon of butter in the pan, which should still be hot. These are best enjoyed warm.

PINEAPPLE–PINE NUT BUTTERMILK CAKE

serves 8 to 10

4 tablespoons (½ stick) plus
   1 teaspoon unsalted butter
2 cups spelt flour
½ cup sorghum flour
1 tablespoon baking powder
½ plus ⅛ teaspoon salt
1½ cups buttermilk

2 large eggs
6 tablespoons honey
Finely grated zest of 3 lemons
1 tablespoon packed chopped
   fresh basil
¼ cup pine nuts, toasted (see
   page 26)

1½ cups sliced pineapple
   (2-inch-long by ¼-inch-wide
   batons)
2 tablespoons plus 2 teaspoons
   raw sugar, such as turbinado

When asked to cover some of the brightest new pastry stars—and their recipes—for a food magazine, I immediately thought of Kristen D. Murray of Portland, Oregon's Måurice, where locals gather for *fika*, a Swedish coffee break. She suggested a pine nut and pineapple torte, engaging in the kind of culinary wordplay I love.

This simple, skillet-friendly buttermilk cake repurposes that ingredient matchup. The versatile base features spelt flour—it's got a wholesome charm plus a pronounced nuttiness. I bring in a bit of sorghum flour, too, for its sweetness. The result is almost like a zucchini bread. I'd have it for *fika*. You might find it even better the next day for breakfast. To present it as more of a dessert, I'd serve it with unsweetened whipped cream. I hope Kristen would approve. This one's for her.

1 Preheat the oven to 375°F with a 10-inch cast-iron skillet placed on a rack in the top third of the oven. In a small saucepan, melt 4 tablespoons of the butter and set aside.

2 In a large bowl, whisk together the flours, baking powder, and salt. In a smaller bowl, whisk together the buttermilk, eggs, and honey. Whisk in the melted butter and zest. Add the wet ingredients to the dry, stirring just to combine. Mix in the basil and pine nuts.

3 Remove the hot skillet from the oven. Add the remaining 1 teaspoon butter to melt and brush it over the bottom and sides of the pan. Scrape the batter into the skillet, spreading it evenly and smoothing the top. Scatter the pineapple over the surface and sprinkle the raw sugar on top.

4 Bake for 30 to 35 minutes, until the top is golden and the center has just set—a cake tester inserted into the center should come out clean, but err on the softer side; it will firm up as it cools. Leave it in the skillet for about 10 minutes before using the Upside-Down Plate Trick (see page 56) to flip it out and serve it pineapple-side up.

CACIO E PEPE SHORTBREAD

serves 10 to 12

½ cup plus 2 teaspoons finely grated Parmesan cheese

½ cup plus 2 teaspoons finely grated Pecorino Romano cheese

2 teaspoons coarsely ground black pepper

1 cup (2 sticks) unsalted butter, at room temperature

½ cup confectioners' sugar

1¼ teaspoons kosher salt

1½ cups all-purpose flour

½ cup semolina flour

1 tablespoon plus 2 teaspoons extra-virgin olive oil

As I get older, I tend to prefer simpler things. This includes chef Mark Ladner's *bavette cacio e pepe* at Lupa, which has few ingredients, but is all about that throat-tickling burn of pepper and the grainy Italian cheese texture against smooth, spaghettilike noodles. Something else I return to again and again is shortbread. The buttery, not-too-sweet, hint-of-salt block is a treat that's served me well from childhood through adulthood.

This classic-pasta-turned-cookie functions much like a biscotti: it goes well with espresso, or even a dessert wine, although I might prefer a glass of Riesling or prosecco myself. It's intended as homage to both Chef Ladner and my friend Caitlin Freeman, who has perfected the art of shortbread, and it might just be my favorite recipe in this cookbook (but you didn't hear that from me).

1　Preheat the oven to 350°F with a 10-inch cast-iron skillet in it.

2　In a small bowl, combine 2 teaspoons each of the Parmesan and pecorino and 1 teaspoon of the pepper. Set aside.

3　In the bowl of a stand mixer fitted with the paddle, beat the butter on low speed for 1 minute or so, until it's smooth and fluffy, like cake frosting. Add the sugar, salt, and remaining 1 teaspoon pepper and mix until combined. Turn off the mixer and, using a rubber spatula, scrape down the sides of the bowl. Set the speed to medium and mix for 4 to 5 minutes more, until the mixture takes on a thick, creamy, almost shiny texture, like mayonnaise.

4   Turn off the mixer and scrape down the sides of the bowl again. Add the flours and mix on low speed to incorporate. Turn off the mixer, scrape down the sides of the bowl one more time, add the remaining ½ cup Parmesan and ½ cup pecorino and mix for 1 minute. Using the rubber spatula, push the dough together to form a ball.

5   Remove the hot skillet from the oven and brush it with 1 teaspoon of the olive oil. Turn the dough into the skillet and, working quickly, using your fingers (but being careful of the hot pan), press the dough into the skillet, pushing it out to fill the edges and flattening it to create an even surface. Brush the top with the remaining 1 tablespoon plus 1 teaspoon olive oil. Sprinkle the dough with the cheese-pepper mixture.

6   Bake the shortbread for 18 to 23 minutes, until the edges begin to brown. The middle should be cooked through, but slightly soft; it will harden as it cools. Let cool for 10 minutes. Use the Upside-Down Plate Trick (see page 56) to flip the shortbread out so it's right-side up. Let cool completely.

7   To serve, divide the shortbread into 10 to 12 wedges. Enjoy it with your afternoon coffee, or, which I encourage, aperitifs, like prosecco, Bellinis, rosé, or whatever you like to drink at cocktail hour.

TOMATO PIE
(WITH APOLOGIES TO HATTIE MAE)
serves 6

DOUGH

1½ cups unbleached all-purpose flour

½ cup almond flour

1 heaping teaspoon fine sea salt

¼ cup plus 1 teaspoon olive oil (see Notes)

¼ cup plus 2 tablespoons cold water

¼ cup pine nuts, toasted (see page 26)

FILLING

½ cup dry sun-dried tomatoes

1 cup mayonnaise (preferably Duke's)

½ cup fresh goat cheese, at room temperature

½ cup grated sharp cheddar cheese

½ cup mixed coarsely chopped fresh oregano leaves, basil, and/or flat-leaf parsley

3 medium beefsteak tomatoes, each cut crosswise into six ¼-inch-thick slices

1 teaspoon kosher salt

½ teaspoon olive oil

1 cup finely diced onions

¼ plus ⅛ teaspoon fine sea salt

¼ plus ⅛ teaspoon freshly ground black pepper

I had never eaten tomato pie—not the one known throughout the American South—until I met chef Elizabeth "Heidi" Trull of Grits and Groceries in South Carolina. Her piping-hot, straight-out-of-the-oven pie was sealed with a thick, blistered cap of cheddar, and when you bit into it, it was creamy, with tomatoes that were burstingly juicy.

Before I left the restaurant, she shoved a collection of recipes into my hand. Inside, I found Hattie Mae's tomato pie. Its namesake, Heidi notes, "was a wonderful lady who took care of us all growing up in Sumter [South Carolina] and this pie makes me think of her and home."

I couldn't wait to make such a nostalgic dish, one that would take me back to my childhood. If I wrote a family cookbook, the chapter on my mother, Nancy, would be titled Sun-Dried Tomatoes, Goat Cheese & Pine Nuts; she adds these ingredients to almost everything.

I associate those things with the 1980s, and I chide my mom for her unwillingness to abandon this dated triumvirate, but the truth is, I kind of love their potency, especially when combined. I took Hattie Mae's tomato pie, and I fused it with a taste of the '80s. It's a concentrated—and I think—dazzling mash-up.

1 **Make the dough:** In a large bowl, whisk together the flours and sea salt. Add the olive oil and, using your hands (or a fork), rub the dry ingredients and oil together to combine, yielding a crumbly mixture. Make a well in the middle and add ¼ cup cold water. Continue to incorporate, using your hands or a fork, until dough clumps begin to form. Add more water, 1 teaspoon at a time, as needed, until the dough comes together.

(RECIPE CONTINUES)

Using the heel of your hand, quickly and gently knead it into a ball, folding the pine nuts in as you go (poke any strays back in), then flatten the dough into a disc.

2   Place a 14-inch square of wax paper on your work surface and put the disc of dough on top of it. Place another piece of wax paper, the same size as the first, on top of the dough. Using a rolling pin, roll the dough into a circle about 10 inches wide and ¼ inch thick as follows: roll from the center, pushing the pin first out, then back, then rotate the dough 45 degrees before again rolling it out, then back. Once the dough is the desired size, transfer it to a plastic freezer bag (keeping it between the sheets of wax paper) and refrigerate for at least 2 hours or up to overnight.

3   **Make the filling:** Soak the sun-dried tomatoes in warm water for 1 hour, timing it so they're done when you're ready to start assembling the pie. Drain, then chop them into bite-size pieces.

4   Preheat the oven to 350°F. In a medium bowl, stir together the mayonnaise, goat cheese, cheddar, and one-third of the mixed herbs. Set the bowl aside.

5   Place the tomato slices on a baking sheet and sprinkle with the kosher salt. Let them sweat for 10 minutes. Meanwhile, take the pie dough out of the refrigerator and let it soften enough to make maneuvering it easier.

6   Preheat a 10-inch cast-iron skillet on the stovetop over low heat for 5 minutes. Rinse the tomato slices under cold water and pat them dry with paper towel.

7   Turn off the burner and brush the olive oil onto the warm pan. Fit the dough into the skillet to form the crust, carefully pushing the edges up against the sides of the pan to create a 1-inch rim. Lay one-third of the tomato slices in the pie shell, followed by one-third of the sun-dried tomatoes, half the onions, and one-third of the mixed herbs. Season with ¼ teaspoon each of the fine sea salt and pepper. Repeat with another layer of each ingredient. Finally, add the remaining tomatoes and sun-dried tomatoes and season with the remaining sea salt and pepper. Spread the mayo mixture over the top and bake for 45 minutes to 1 hour, until the crust is golden and the top is golden brown and bubbling.

8   Serve hot. It's great at room temperature, too. Refrigerate leftovers and eat them cold the next day. Don't even bother with reheating.

NOTES

- You can prepare the crust the day before and assemble and bake the pie in record time, for a quick weeknight dinner. And you can make it year-round, even when tomatoes aren't in their prime.

- Thanks to olive oil, this pie dough is less flaky and more crackerlike to handle the weight and moisture of the tomatoes.

FIG-ALMOND CLAFOUTI WITH SAFFRON SYRUP

serves 8

BATTER

3 large eggs

¼ cup sugar, plus 1 scant tablespoon for tossing

¼ cup unbleached all-purpose flour

1 tablespoon plus 1 teaspoon semolina (see Note)

¼ teaspoon salt

1⅓ cups half-and-half

½ teaspoon almond extract

½ teaspoon vanilla extract

Generous pinch of saffron (or ⅛ teaspoon)

2 cups sliced black figs (⅛ inch thin)

1 teaspoon butter

½ cup sliced almonds

Crème fraîche, for serving

Saffron Syrup, for serving (recipe follows)

Clafouti (*clah-foo-tee*) is easier to make than it is to pronounce, and it's a cast-iron regular. It allows you to whip up a quick-as-can-be batter, pour it over whatever seasonal fruit is at its peak, and bake the whole thing. But see, I've never liked the southern French confection much. I find it eggy, in the wrong way—it reminds me of overcooked scrambled eggs. So I created a clafouti that I could love, with more texture, thanks to granular semolina. I sexed it up with my favorite fruit, figs, and one of the world's greatest luxuries, musky, warm, gold-staining saffron. Then I topped it with a sauce created by baking angel Elizabeth Quijada of Abraço in the East Village: a honey-flavored simple syrup infused with more of those extravagant crimson threads. Now, it seems, I love clafouti.

1 Preheat the oven to 400°F with a 10-inch cast-iron skillet in it.

2 In a large bowl, whisk together the eggs and ¼ cup of the sugar until well combined and frothy, then add the flour, semolina, salt, half-and-half, almond extract, and vanilla. Stir with the whisk to incorporate, trying to get as smooth a batter as possible. Add the saffron and whisk gently to combine, trying not to break the spice threads. In a medium bowl, gently toss the figs with the remaining scant tablespoon sugar.

3 Remove the hot skillet from the oven and add the butter. Once it melts, brush it over the surface of the pan to coat. Layer the figs over the surface of the pan, being careful not to burn your fingers on the hot metal, and scatter the almonds on top. Carefully pour

(RECIPE CONTINUES)

the batter over the almonds and figs so they aren't displaced. Bake until the surface of the clafouti has puffed up and is golden, its edges beginning to brown, about 30 minutes.

4   You can let the clafouti cool completely, but it tastes insanely good warm, too. Serve it out of the skillet, topping each slice with a dollop of crème fraîche and about a tablespoon of the saffron syrup drizzled over it. It will immediately begin to deflate once it's out of the oven; that's normal. Any leftover clafouti can be stored in an airtight container overnight and eaten at room temperature the next day.

> **NOTE**   Milled from hard durum wheat, *semolina* is not the same thing as *semolina flour;* the latter is more finely ground than the former. If you can't find semolina, look for a coarsely ground semolina flour or, if necessary, use the standard variety. It's okay! (It's still relatively grittier than a soft flour like all-purpose or Italian "00".) You might also try substituting a medium- or coarse-ground cornmeal.

SAFFRON SYRUP
makes about 1 cup

1 cup sugar
½ cup boiling water
¼ teaspoon saffron threads (or less, for subtler flavor)
¼ cup honey

1   Stir all the ingredients together until the sugar dissolves and the syrup takes on a brilliant yellow color. Set aside until ready to serve.

2   Leftovers can be used on yogurt and vanilla ice cream, or poured over pound cake, and can be stored in a sealed container in the refrigerator for up to 2 weeks. Alternatively, you can halve the ingredients and make just enough for the clafouti.

CARROT-CURRANT CROSTATA

serves 6

CRUST

1 cup unbleached all-purpose
  flour, plus more for dusting
½ cup buckwheat flour
½ teaspoon kosher salt
1½ teaspoons celery seeds
10 tablespoons unsalted butter,
  cut into ½-inch cubes and
  frozen (see Note)
¼ cup ice water, plus more as
  needed

FILLING

2 bunches of medium carrots,
  cut into 1-inch batons (thicker
  pieces should be split; about
  3½ cups)
1 tablespoon olive oil
½ teaspoon celery seeds
½ teaspoon cumin seeds

1¼ teaspoons kosher salt, plus
  more to taste
1½ teaspoons pomegranate
  molasses
¼ cup currants

1 large egg

Some of the best culinary inventions have come out of using a few basic pantry items. I had three in mind when I started on this rustic-style tart—celery, raisins, and peanut butter. They form the children's snack known as ants on a log, and sometimes carrot sticks stand in for the celery "logs." I worked the seeds responsible for those fibrous green stalks into the crust, which is made with complementary, grassy buckwheat flour. I lined the pastry base with peanut butter and put the orange root veg in the filling with currants; they're smaller and more tart than raisins, and I prefer them in savory dishes. I liked everything about this crostata, except for the peanut butter. It overpowered the rest. I could have stuck with it, stubbornly clinging to the cleverness of the original reference. But that's another rule of cooking: flavor trumps. I removed the offending ingredient, and I had a real winner.

1 Start the crust: In a food processor, pulse together the flours, salt, and celery seeds a few times just to mix. Add the cubed butter and pulse again, until it breaks down into pea-size pieces and the mixture resembles a coarse meal. With the motor running, slowly trickle the ice water into the food processor, just until the dough comes together. Don't add too much water or overmix the dough; it should take 30 seconds, tops. Test it by squeezing a bit between your thumb and index finger; if it's too crumbly, add 1 to 2 teaspoons more ice water, pulsing the machine this time to quickly incorporate the water. Test the dough again, continuing until it's the right consistency.

2 Turn the dough out onto a lightly floured surface, press it gently into a flat, round disc,

and double wrap in plastic wrap. Refrigerate for 2 to 4 hours, or up to overnight.

3   **Meanwhile, make the filling:** Preheat the oven to 450°F. In a medium bowl, combine the carrots and the olive oil, tossing or stirring to coat evenly.

4   Preheat a 10-inch cast-iron skillet on the stove, gradually raising the heat from low to medium-high. When the pan is hot, add the celery seeds and cumin seeds. Toast them for about a minute, shaking the pan continuously, until they release their fragrance and just begin to color. Transfer the toasted seeds to a spice grinder and grind them. Add the ground spices and 1 teaspoon of the salt to the bowl with the carrots and toss or stir to mix together.

5   Spread the carrots out in one layer on a baking sheet. Roast for 15 to 20 minutes, until they begin to shrivel and caramelize.

6   Transfer the roasted carrots to a medium bowl. Add the pomegranate molasses and toss to coat evenly. Add the currants and mix together. Sprinkle the remaining ¼ teaspoon salt over the mixture and combine; taste and add more salt as needed. Set aside to cool.

7   Reduce the oven temperature to 400°F. Take the chilled dough out of the refrigerator and let it rest for about 10 minutes.

8   In the meantime, in a small bowl, whisk the egg, then whisk in 2 tablespoons water to make an egg wash.

9   **Finish the crust:** Place the dough on a lightly floured work surface and, using a lightly floured rolling pin, roll it out to a circle 10 to 11 inches in diameter, rotating it 45 degrees after every few rolls, and flipping it over once or twice to get an even thickness. Don't worry if it's not a perfect circle.

10 Have the skillet near your rolling station so you can easily transfer the rolled dough to the pan, laying it down so you have a relatively even amount of crust coming up on all sides. Spread the carrot-currant mixture over the crust, leaving a border about 1½ inches around the perimeter. Fold the excess dough edges up and around the filling, making pleats to hold the crust together and secure the filling. Brush the dough with the egg wash.

11 Bake for about 40 minutes, until the crust is golden brown. Let the crostata rest for 20 minutes before serving it straight from the skillet or, using a spatula, gently lifting it out of the pan onto a serving plate.

Working with Butter

Unless otherwise advised, if I'm making a butter crust, I cut my butter into ½-inch cubes. If I am going to use a machine like a food processor or stand mixer, I freeze my butter. Those appliances can cut through butter a lot faster than my hands can, but at the same time, their engines add heat to the dough. Just remember, your goal is to keep the butter cold, to distribute it evenly, and to quit while you're ahead.

SORGHUM BISCUITS

makes 7 or 8 biscuits

1¼ cups all-purpose flour, plus
    more for dusting
¼ cup sorghum flour
1½ teaspoons baking powder
Scant ½ teaspoon salt

⅛ teaspoon baking soda
8 tablespoons (1 stick) unsalted
    butter, cut into ½-inch cubes
    and chilled

¼ cup crème fraîche
¼ cup buttermilk, plus more
    as needed

Biscuit recipes strike me as extremely personal—proprietarily so. Even when people adhere to a family formula passed down from one generation to the next, their biscuits are always their own, a little different thanks to a more generous pinch of salt or a lighter touch with the dough. I wanted to re-create a biscuit that would showcase all the things I learned in a baking class taught by former Husk pastry chef Lisa Donovan, with just a few tiny ingredient changes that would put my imprint on it. A Southern crop, sorghum is known best for the thick, slightly sour, sugary syrup it produces. The sweet-smelling ancient cereal grain can also be ground into flour for baking. Even though it comprises a small one-fifth of the flour content in this recipe, I think it makes a flavorful difference.

My second alteration is more controversial. I put crème fraîche in my biscuits! Those living below the Mason-Dixon Line will probably take issue with this and categorize these as biscuit-flavored scones. I don't care. I'm not Southern—my biscuit was born in New York City, where anything goes, as long as it tastes good. And that it does.

1. In a large bowl, combine the flours, baking powder, salt, and baking soda and use your hands to mix it all together. Add all but 2 of the butter cubes to the dry ingredients. Working quickly, incorporate the butter by smearing it into the dry ingredients with your fingers, one small pile at a time, making sure all the dry ingredients have been introduced to the butter so that you end up with something resembling a coarse crumble.

2. Using a spoon or knife, drop the crème fraîche into the bowl in dollops, scattering them over the surface. Begin to swirl your hands through the mixture, using your fingers to incorporate the crème fraîche and form clumps. You will still have a relatively dry, loose, crumbly pile with doughlike pockets beginning to come together. Begin pouring the buttermilk over the surface of the mixture, continuing to use your fingers to integrate the wet and dry ingredients and form a sticky dough. You may not need all the buttermilk (you don't want your dough to be too wet). Alternatively, if the mixture is still too dry, add a bit more buttermilk, as needed, 1 teaspoon at a time. Using your fingers more than your palms, bring the dough together so it's thoroughly incorporated, working it without kneading it, being careful not to overwork the dough.

3. Dump the dough out onto a floured work surface and pat it into a ¾-inch-thick rectangle. Press—without twisting—a 2¼-inch biscuit cutter straight down into the dough to cut out rounds, getting as many as you can out of the initial rectangle of dough. Pile the scraps on top of one another in layers and pat them out to form another rectangle; cut as many more rounds from it as you can. Repeat until there is no dough left.

4. Lay the biscuits flat in groups of 3 or 4 between sheets of wax paper, and place in a plastic bag or sealable container. Refrigerate for at least 1 hour. You can also leave them overnight.

5. When you are ready to bake the biscuits, preheat the oven to 375°F with a 10-inch cast-iron skillet in it. Once the oven is hot enough, remove the pan and add the 2 remaining butter cubes to it. Let the butter melt and tilt to coat. Place the biscuits in the pan, filling it up. Bake the biscuits for about 20 minutes, until the tops have a light golden hue and a cake tester inserted into the center of a biscuit comes out clean. Grab 'em while they're hot—or at the very least, warm.

NOTE You can melt the butter in your skillet right before you put it in the oven to preheat. After you set the butter aside to cool for the batter, quickly wipe out the pan, no need to rinse it. Then place it in the oven.

BANANA-MATCHA BUTTER MOCHI CAKE

serves 10 to 12

3 cups mochiko flour

2¼ teaspoons baking powder

2¼ cups sugar

1 tablespoon matcha powder

1½ teaspoons salt

3 large eggs

1⅛ cups coconut milk

1⅛ cups evaporated milk

1½ teaspoons vanilla extract

6 tablespoons (¾ stick) unsalted
butter, melted and cooled
(see Note)

2 not-too-ripe bananas, sliced
crosswise into ¼-inch-thick
coins, then quartered (about
1½ cups)

My adaptation of *butter mochi*, a popular Hawaiian snack, epitomizes what I like to call a party trick. You can make it in a jiffy, with little paraphernalia, and it will surprise whomever you serve it to. For many, it'll be a first taste of *mochiko*—the flour made from the same short-grain, glutinous sweet rice pounded into a paste and molded into mochi. If you've had the dumplinglike Japanese treats, you're familiar with their distinct, bizarrely delightful, gummy texture. This cake carries it to an unobvious albeit semi-logical conclusion—it delivers that chewy, comforting experience in warm, just-baked form. Matcha's bright, freshly-mown-lawn color and aroma transform the dessert into something remarkable. The powdered tea dyes the batter an unforgettable shade of *KAPOW*, while its astringency serves as a foil for the cake's extreme sweetness. Rather than using overripe bananas (like you would in banana bread), ones in their younger state help temper the cake's saccharinity instead of increasing it. Sliced into bite-size pieces, the fruit remains intact, a final surprise.

1   Preheat the oven to 350°F with a 10-inch cast-iron skillet in it.

2   In a large bowl, using a wooden spoon, stir together the mochiko flour, baking powder, sugar, matcha powder, and salt. In a medium bowl, whisk together the eggs, coconut milk, evaporated milk, vanilla, and melted butter. Pour the wet ingredients into the dry, stirring with a wooden spoon until you have a green batter. Make sure all the dry ingredients at the bottom of the bowl have been completely integrated. (Don't worry about overmixing this batter.) Fold in the bananas.

3   Pour the batter into the pan and bake for 1 hour, until the top of the cake is golden and just browned around the edges. Enjoy warm, out of the pan, or at room temperature. The cake is best stored at room temperature, wrapped in plastic wrap or in a sealed container for up to 3 days. Zap it in the microwave for that warm, just-baked effect.

BERRY UPSIDE-DOWN CHOCOLATE CAKE

serves 12

BERRY TOPPING

1 pint blackberries

½ cup granulated sugar

2 tablespoons light brown sugar

2 tablespoons Chambord

1 tablespoon unsalted butter

CAKE

1¼ cups unbleached all-purpose
flour

¼ cup unsweetened cocoa
powder (see Notes)

1 teaspoon baking powder

¼ teaspoon salt

⅔ cup (3 ounces) bittersweet
(around 65%) chocolate,
chopped

6 tablespoons (¾ stick) unsalted
butter, cut into 12 pieces

2 tablespoons hot water, just off
the boil (see Notes)

1¼ cups granulated sugar

2 large eggs, at room temperature

1½ teaspoons vanilla extract

½ cup buttermilk

1 pint raspberries

1 tablespoon fresh lemon juice

Vanilla ice cream, crème fraîche,
or freshly whipped cream, for
serving

People presume upside-down cakes to have a vanilla or golden base. Why not chocolate? I asked the one person you can always count on for a perfect upside-down cake: Gina DePalma. The former pastry chef of Babbo and an Italian American, she had an encyclopedia's worth of information on the desserts of Italy stored in her brain, and she wrote about or baked most of them. As you may have guessed, this cake is not Italian. It calls for blackberries, which are on hand year-round and, as Gina said, "are bold enough to stand up to chocolate." They're complex—sweet and juicy, but also tart and sour. Here they cook down into a wonderful syrupy quagmire flavored with Chambord to bring out their succulence. That black raspberry spirit is crucial as far as I'm concerned, but you can play around with other liqueurs or skip it altogether.

1 **Prepare the berry topping:** Preheat a 10-inch cast-iron skillet on the stovetop, gradually raising the heat from low to medium. Place the blackberries in the pan with the granulated and brown sugars and the Chambord. Using a wooden spoon, crush the berries slightly to release some of their juices. Cook, stirring continuously and adjusting the heat as necessary to prevent scorching, for about 25 minutes, until the berries have taken on a jamlike texture; it should be glossy and not watery, but not tight. You'll know it's ready when you drag the wooden spoon through it and the mixture pulls away and leaves tracks that just begin to hold. Turn off the heat and add the butter, stirring it in as it melts to combine. Set aside to cool.

(RECIPE CONTINUES)

2   **Make the cake:** Preheat the oven to 325°F. Sift the flour, cocoa powder, baking powder, and salt together into a medium bowl. Using a whisk, stir to break up any clumps of cocoa powder.

3   In a medium heatproof bowl set over a wide pan of gently simmering water (or using a double boiler), melt the chocolate and butter together, whisking frequently. Whisk the hot water into the chocolate mixture and remove the bowl from the pan of simmering water. Whisk 1 cup of the granulated sugar into the chocolate mixture (it will get grainy). Whisk the eggs in, one at a time, followed by the vanilla.

4   Whisk half the dry ingredients into the chocolate mixture, followed by the buttermilk, then whisk in the remaining dry ingredients. Switch to a rubber spatula at the very end to make sure you've scraped the sides of the bowl and the ingredients are thoroughly combined.

5   In a medium bowl, gently toss together the raspberries, lemon juice, and remaining ¼ cup granulated sugar to coat the berries. Scatter the raspberries evenly over the surface of the cooled blackberry compote in the skillet.

6   Using an offset spatula, carefully spread the cake batter over the berries. Bake the cake for about 40 minutes, rotating the skillet 180 degrees halfway through baking, until just cooked through. A cake tester or fork inserted into the center should come out clean, and the berry juices should be bubbling up at the sides.

7   Let the cake cool in the skillet for 15 minutes before unmolding it, carefully, while it's still warm. Use a butter knife to loosen the sides of the cake from the pan, then use the Upside-Down Plate Trick (see page 56) to flip it out. Slice it into 12 wedges and serve it with vanilla ice cream, crème fraîche, or freshly whipped cream (sweetened or not).

NOTES

- For this recipe, use the best-quality Dutch-process cocoa powder you can find—the darker, the better. An all-purpose variety like King Arthur's Triple Cocoa Blend, which combines Dutch-process, natural, and black powders, will also work. (Good to know: If a chocolate recipe calls for baking powder, the general rule is to go Dutch. If it has baking soda, use natural cocoa powder.)

- "Off the boil" refers to liquid that has been brought to a boil, then left for just a couple of minutes to cool slightly. For this recipe, you can boil some water and let it sit for 2 to 3 minutes. You don't need to take its temperature, but if you did, you'd see it was somewhere between 195° and 205°F.

DOUBLE CHOCOLATE SCONES WITH CRYSTALLIZED GINGER

makes 10 to 12 scones

8 tablespoons (1 stick) plus 1 teaspoon unsalted butter, per batch

1 large egg

¾ cup heavy cream

1 teaspoon vanilla extract

1¼ cups unbleached all-purpose flour, plus more for dusting

½ cup chestnut flour

¼ cup best-quality unsweetened Dutch-process cocoa powder

3 tablespoons sugar

1 tablespoon baking powder

¼ teaspoon salt

½ cup semisweet chocolate chunks or chocolate chips (see Note)

3 to 4 tablespoons finely chopped crystallized ginger, to taste

The ideal scone should be moist enough that the clotted cream served with it is an option, not a necessity. It should be barely sweet, and that sweetness should derive, mostly, from its fat. What a scone is not, as a matter of course, is chocolate. It might have chocolate chips in it, but you don't see a whole lot of scones made from chocolate dough. That's what I wanted—a perfect chocolate scone. I wanted this thing to show the world that neither scones nor chocolate treats need be so sugary; that, when combined, the natural sweetness of butter and cream and luscious promise of the cocoa bean are enough.

When figuring out this recipe, I followed Dorie Greenspan's method. I carefully studied how much flour, butter, sugar, and cream she uses for her scone dough, and tweaked it to accommodate cocoa powder, which accounts for part of the flour content. I also took out some more of the all-purpose flour, replacing it with sweet and nutty chestnut flour. Chestnut, chocolate, and ginger are a terrific trio, by the way.

1   Cut 8 tablespoons of the butter into ½-inch cubes and chill them in the refrigerator for at least 1 hour.

2   Preheat the oven to 400°F with a 10-inch cast-iron skillet in it.

3   In a small bowl, stir together the egg, cream, and vanilla to combine. In a large bowl, using a whisk, mix together the flours, cocoa powder, sugar, baking powder, and salt.

4   Dump the chilled butter into the bowl with the flour mixture and, with your fingers, toss the cubes to coat. Using either your hands (fingertips, specifically) or a pastry cutter, break the butter up and rub it into the ingredients to incorporate until you get what resembles a coarse meal. Work quickly, while the butter is cold. Don't worry if it doesn't look uniform; you want the butter to be evenly

(RECIPE CONTINUES)

distributed, but it should range in size from flat oatlike flakes to small pea-size pebbles.

5   Pour in the egg mixture and, using a fork, work it into the dry ingredients, just until the dough comes together. Add the chocolate chunks and the ginger, using more or less to taste, and, with your hands, gently knead the dough in the bowl to simultaneously integrate those mix-ins and smooth it out, making sure any remaining dry ingredients stuck to the bottom of the bowl have been worked in and the liquid is thoroughly incorporated. The dough should be wet and sticky. Don't overwork it.

6   Turn the dough out onto a lightly floured work surface and, using a bench scraper, split it in two. Take one half, pat it into a disc about 5 inches wide, and cut it into 6 wedges, each about 2½ inches wide. Do the same with the second disc. Because it's wet, the dough may be a little difficult to maneuver; just work quickly and deliberately and you'll be fine. If you like a more generously portioned scone with a bit more heft and height, cut each of the discs into 5 wedges instead of 6.

7   Remove the hot skillet from the oven and melt the remaining 1 teaspoon butter in it, tilting the pan to coat. Place half the dough wedges in the pan and bake for about 20 minutes, until the tops are just firm, but not rock-solid.

8   You can refrigerate the remaining raw scones if you plan to bake them right after the first group for a full batch, back-to-back. Alternatively, you can freeze the unbaked scones. You don't need to defrost them before baking them, but you should keep them in the oven a couple of minutes longer. Bake as directed above, melting a teaspoon of butter in the skillet before adding the wedges and putting them in the oven. If you want to bake them in advance, once they cool to room temperature, wrap them tightly in a layer of plastic wrap followed by aluminum foil and put them in the freezer right away. They'll keep for up to 2 months and can be reheated in the oven at 350°F, uncovered, for up to 10 minutes.

Kneading by Machine

Whereas in the recipe for Date, Onion & Fontina Scones (page 82), I relied on a stand mixer, for these, Dorie-style, I use my hands. Both lead to success. You could also use a food processor; if you did, you would mix the dry ingredients in the machine, then pulse the butter in until it was broken down into pea-size crumbs. At that point, you'd transfer the mixture to a bowl, before folding in the chocolate chips and ginger. You would then stir in the wet ingredients to form a smooth dough.

NOTE   I prefer chopping chocolate bars into chunks to using semisweet chocolate chips, because I like a less-sweet chocolate; for this recipe, I'd go with a 62 to 68% chocolate. If you're less keen on dark chocolate, choose one with a lower cocoa percentage, or just use old-fashioned chocolate chips.

PB&C OATMEAL SKILLET COOKIE

makes 2 large cookies

⅓ cup plus 1 tablespoon lard, plus 1 teaspoon per batch

1 cup unsweetened coconut flakes

⅓ cup natural smooth peanut butter

8 tablespoons (1 stick) unsalted butter, cut into ½-inch cubes and chilled

4 ounces cream cheese, at room temperature

⅓ cup granulated sugar

¾ cup packed dark brown sugar

2 large eggs

1 teaspoon vanilla extract

2 cups unbleached all-purpose flour

1 teaspoon baking powder

½ teaspoon baking soda

1½ teaspoons plus ½ teaspoon flake sea salt, per batch

2 cups old-fashioned rolled oats

Skillet cookies bring out the kid in all of us. I have memories of reaching my small hands into a pan full of hot, crispy-edged, mushy-middled, M&M's-filled dough, its giant size making it seem naughty, like watching an R-rated movie without an adult chaperone. My inner child still loves those extra-large treats, only she'd prefer an oatmeal cookie. So that's what I gave her. Levain Bakery on the Upper West Side of Manhattan produces my favorite example. It's massive, extremely soft, and dense; it has the thickness of a plump scone and a craggy, crunchy top. Strangely enough, it isn't chock-full of oats, but rather the grains are interspersed more the way nuts might be in a cookie. No one has ever been able to precisely replicate Levain's dough, but one thing everyone agrees on is that cream cheese is involved. That secured it a place in my recipe. I also wanted some coconut and peanut butter in there. The lard, which I added for flavor and to dilute the grainy peanut butter, cuts any excess sugariness.

When I tasted my creation, it reminded me of the inside of a Reese's Pieces candy, with a little pop of salt. It's cakier than a typical oatmeal cookie, but it's perfectly crispy on the outside. Once it cools, it becomes crumbly, almost like a sablé, and that makes it an excellent candidate for a fruit crisp topping (page 201). Make one to serve hot, and freeze the other half of the dough for another time, when you have the distinct longing for an oatmeal cookie, which, surely, from here on in, you will.

1 Preheat a 10-inch cast-iron skillet on the stovetop, gradually raising the heat from low to medium-high. Add 1 tablespoon of the lard. Once the fat is melted and hot, add the coconut flakes and toast them, stirring continuously, for up to 4 minutes, until they're golden brown. Transfer the coconut flakes to a plate and set aside. Wipe out the skillet.

2   Return the skillet to the stove over medium-high heat and add ⅓ cup of the lard. Once it's melted, turn off the heat and let it cool slightly in the skillet, for about 10 minutes. Put the peanut butter in a small bowl and add the melted lard. Stir them together to completely combine, smoothing the peanut butter so there are no lumps. Wipe out the skillet.

3   Measure out ½ cup of the peanut butter mixture and set it aside. (You may have a tablespoon or two extra; it can be used in place of an equal amount of butter in another recipe.)

4   In the bowl of a stand mixer fitted with the paddle, beat the butter, cream cheese, and the ½ cup peanut butter mixture on low speed for about 1 minute, just until it becomes creamy. Add the sugars and continue to beat for 2 minutes more, until it takes on a butterscotch tone and is fairly aerated. You don't want to overbeat it. Add the eggs and vanilla and beat for about 30 seconds to incorporate, being careful not to overbeat. Turn off the mixer and, using a rubber spatula, scrape down the sides of the bowl.

5   In a medium bowl, whisk together the flour, baking powder, baking soda, and 1½ teaspoons of the salt. Add the oats and whisk to incorporate. Add the dry ingredients to the batter in the stand mixer and mix on low speed to combine. You might need to pause and scrape down the sides of the bowl at some point during this process. When the batter is thoroughly mixed, use a wooden spoon to stir in the toasted coconut.

6   Cover the bowl with plastic wrap and stick it in the refrigerator for 30 minutes to 1 hour.

7   Meanwhile, preheat the oven to 375°F with the skillet in it. When the dough has chilled, remove the hot skillet from the oven, add the 1 teaspoon lard, and tilt to coat.

8   Using a spatula, scrape half the dough out into the skillet and press it in, using your fingers when necessary (but being careful of the hot pan), to fill the pan. Sprinkle the surface with the remaining ½ teaspoon salt and bake for 15 to 16 minutes, until the top is golden and the cookie appears just set. Let the cookie sit in the skillet for a minute or two when you take it out of the oven, then use the Upside-Down Plate Trick (see page 56) to turn it onto a plate and then transfer it to a wire rack to cool. If you can't stand the wait, you can eat it straight out of the pan while it's warm.

9   If you want to make the second cookie right away, keep the second half of the dough in the mixing bowl and put it in the refrigerator while the first half bakes. Otherwise, you can freeze the remaining dough until you're ready to bake it. It will keep for a couple of months wrapped tightly in plastic wrap. Let it defrost in the refrigerator before baking, following the directions above, using 1 teaspoon of lard in the hot skillet and sprinkling ½ teaspoon flake sea salt over the top of the dough.

FAT THIN BARS

makes 16 small bars

CRUST

5 cups original Wheat Thins
    (about one and a half
    9.1-ounce boxes)

¼ cup plus 1 tablespoon packed
    dark brown sugar

10 tablespoons (1¼ sticks) plus
    1 teaspoon unsalted butter

TOPPING

1⅓ cups best-quality
    butterscotch chips

⅓ cup white miso paste

½ cup plus 2 tablespoons light
    corn syrup

3½ tablespoons unsalted butter

¼ teaspoon salt

2 cups raw unsalted cashew
    pieces, toasted (see page 26),
    or unsalted roasted cashews

1 teaspoon fleur de sel, plus
    more to taste

Everyone has her weakness; her "betcha can't eat just one" potato chip or "get your own box" cheese cracker. Pringles, Doritos, Triscuits, Cheetos, Cheez Doodles, Sun Chips, I've tried them all, and then some—who else here can say she ate Keebler Tato Skins and appreciated their *baked potato appeal*? With all that sampling, my salty-crunchy drug of choice has always been Wheat Thins. I vowed to put them in a piecrust one day. Then I tried Amy Scherber's butterscotch-cashew bars at her bakery, Amy's Breads, and had a slight change of plans. Those crackers, saltier than the original buttery base, or the obvious graham-cracker alternative, would offer a better contrast, in both flavor and consistency, to the tawny, gooey-sweet topping.

    This new crust is thick, as it should be, and you get sharp shards of the caramelized wheat crackers snapping against your teeth, intermingling with the soft, molten butterscotch and the gentle crunch of the nuts. I gave the topping an upgrade to match, incorporating

white miso paste and fleur de sel to balance its sugar with some saline complexity. The payoff is a grown-up candy bar for those of us who will never be too old for junk food. If you want to make it even more adult, you can try using a flavored salt—rosemary or chocolate, for example.

1 **Make the crust:** Preheat the oven to 350°F with a 10-inch cast-iron skillet placed on the middle rack.

2 Place the Wheat Thins and brown sugar in the bowl of a food processor. Pulse a few times to begin to break down the crackers, then process continuously for about 20 seconds until they've been mostly crushed into crumbs—you should have some jagged fragments amid the crumbs, which will yield a crunchier, rougher, more satisfying texture. Transfer the crumbs to a medium bowl and set aside.

(RECIPE CONTINUES)

3   In a small saucepan, melt 10 tablespoons
    of the butter and pour it over the crumbs.
    Using a rubber spatula, stir the mixture to
    combine, making sure all the crumbs are
    evenly coated. They should look wet and hold
    together when clumped in your fist.

4   Remove the hot skillet from the oven and
    place the remaining 1 teaspoon butter in
    it. Let the butter melt and brush it over the
    surface of the pan to coat. Pour the crumb
    mixture into the skillet and use your fingers
    to press the crust base evenly into the pan,
    being careful to avoid the hot edges. Bake
    for about 12 minutes, until the crust has
    caramelized and smells fragrantly toasted.

5   **Meanwhile, make the topping:** In a medium
    saucepan, combine the butterscotch chips,
    miso paste, corn syrup, butter, salt, and
    2 tablespoons water. Cook over medium heat,
    stirring continuously, for about 5 minutes,
    until the chips have melted and the mixture
    has just begun to simmer and bubble around
    the edges of the saucepan. Turn off the heat
    and whisk the molten butterscotch mixture
    to smooth any remaining clumps of miso
    paste. Add the cashews, using a rubber
    spatula to stir them into the topping.

6   With the spatula, spread the mixture over
    the baked crust. Try to distribute the
    topping evenly over the crust, extending it
    to the edges, but don't worry if you can't;
    it'll spread out during baking. Sprinkle the
    fleur de sel evenly over the surface. Return
    the skillet to the oven and bake for about
    15 minutes, or until the topping is a rich
    brown and bubbling.

7   Let it cool completely in the skillet, at least
    an hour, before running a butter knife
    around the rim of the pan to detach the crust
    and/or butterscotch topping. Then, using the
    Upside-Down Plate Trick (see page 56), flip
    it onto a plate, then onto another plate so it's
    right-side up. Using a sharp knife, slice it
    into 16 small bars.

ALMOND BUTTER & RHUBARB TART

serves 10 to 12

ROASTED RHUBARB FILLING

5⅓ cups trimmed rhubarb, cut
    into 1-inch chunks
¾ cup plus 2 teaspoons
    granulated sugar
3½ tablespoons tapioca flour
    (see Notes)
Zest of 1 medium orange

OAT CRUST

6 tablespoons (¾ stick) plus
    1 teaspoon unsalted butter
¾ cup packed dark brown sugar
¾ cup unbleached all-purpose
    flour
1½ cups old-fashioned rolled oats
⅓ teaspoon baking soda
1 teaspoon salt

ALMOND CRUMB TOPPING

⅔ cup packed dark brown sugar
⅔ cup unbleached all-purpose
    flour
3 tablespoons sliced raw almonds
3 tablespoons old-fashioned
    rolled oats
1 teaspoon salt
4 tablespoons (½ stick) unsalted
    butter, cut into cubes and
    chilled

6 tablespoons almond butter

I like how Gillian Shaw's mind works. At Black Jet Baking Co. in San Francisco, she revamps old-fashioned American baked goods using seasonal produce. She turns out raspberry jam bars with a brown sugar crumble topping. They have the perfect amount of piquant, thick, sticky fruit and a toffeed, buttery oat crust. They would, I imagined, translate well to a tart and could be made in a cast-iron skillet. So I thought I'd ask her if they could be adapted, accordingly, and taken in a new direction with almond butter. Then she mentioned "strawberries and rhubarb," and it was game over for jam. I saw no need for the berries, either.

I don't know why we don't let rhubarb perform solo more often. Gillian instructed me to roast the tangy, herbaceous vegetable first, with orange zest and sugar. This alone would have been enough. You could have it with a big old plop-down of whipped cream or a scoop of vanilla ice cream. Better to go for the tart, though. For me, it's the creamy, thick almond butter that makes it truly indulgent, but at the same time, it's the thing that cuts through the richness of the rest of this crunchy, sweet dessert.

(RECIPE CONTINUES)

1   **Make the rhubarb filling:** Preheat the oven to 350°F. In a large bowl, toss together the rhubarb, sugar, tapioca flour, and zest. Set aside for about 20 minutes.

2   Place the rhubarb mixture in a medium-large Pyrex or ceramic baking dish and bake for 20 minutes. Don't worry if not all the sugar melts—it will finish cooking in the pie. Remove the dish from the oven and set it aside to cool; leave the oven on.

3   **Make the oat crust:** In a small saucepan, melt 6 tablespoons of the butter over medium-high heat. Set aside.

4   In a medium bowl, combine the brown sugar, flour, oats, baking soda, and salt and use your hands to mix them together, breaking up any clumps of brown sugar. Pour the melted butter over the dry ingredients and, using a spatula, thoroughly incorporate to get a mixture that resembles wet sand.

5   Preheat a 10-inch cast-iron skillet over low heat. Once it's warm, add the remaining 1 teaspoon butter and, as it melts, brush it over the bottom and sides of the skillet. Press the oat mixture into the skillet, pushing some of it about halfway up the sides; the base should be about ½ inch thick.

Bake the oat crust for about 15 minutes, until it turns a light golden brown. Remove from the oven and set aside; leave the oven on.

6   **Make the almond crumb topping:** In the bowl of a stand mixer fitted with the paddle, mix the brown sugar, flour, almonds, oats, and salt on low speed for about 20 seconds to combine. Add the cubed butter piece by piece and continue to mix for about 1 minute, until you have a crumbly topping. Watch it carefully; you don't want the butter to cream, or to be left with a ball of dough. There will be chunks of butter left—this is okay.

7   **Assemble the tart:** Using an offset spatula, a small rubber spatula, or the back of a spoon, gently spread the almond butter over the oat crust to cover it evenly. Spoon the roasted rhubarb over the layer of almond butter, including some of the roasting juices in each spoonful, but being careful not to oversaturate the pie (use up to ⅔ cup of the liquid). Generously pile the almond crumb topping over the fruit, using your fingers to distribute it evenly over the surface of the pie.

8   Bake the tart for 20 minutes, then cover with aluminum foil and bake for 20 minutes more. Let cool for 30 minutes before serving.

NOTES

- Feel free to skip the rhubarb filling and use your favorite preserves (raspberry, strawberry, blueberry, apricot, peach, or even marmalade). Start with about the same amount of jam as almond butter and add more to taste. You could also try this with another ripe fruit, like apricots, depending on the season.

- Gillian prefers tapioca flour as a thickening agent, as opposed to cornstarch, because it doesn't create the weird congealed texture that cornstarch can yield. She uses tapioca flour in all pie fillings except for apple, when she uses all-purpose flour.

HALVA FUDGE BARS

makes 16 bars

1 cup (2 sticks) plus 1 teaspoon
    butter
2 large eggs
1¼ teaspoons salt

1 cup packed dark brown sugar
⅔ cup date syrup
1½ teaspoons vanilla extract
2 cups teff flour

1 cup fried marcona almonds
1 cup packed halva

I originally called these blondies. They have the necessary brown sugar and butter associated with cocoa-free brownies. But they're not blonde, they're maroon, thanks to an Ethiopian staple, teff flour, and, indirectly, the Middle Eastern sesame confection, halva. Blondies are frequently dry. It becomes egregious when, to that dryness, you bring an even drier accoutrement like halva. I added a dark burgundy-colored date syrup to create an extra moist batter. By pulling out the pan while the center is still gooey and barely set and the top is crisp, you achieve the baking equivalent of searing a piece of steak on cast iron: a solid crust with a "rare" inside. Like the meat, the dough won't stop cooking once it's out of the oven. The results are *so* moist, "blondie" isn't a good enough label. My halva miracle is more like fudge, and so I changed its name appropriately.

1 Preheat the oven to 350°F with a 10-inch cast-iron skillet placed on a rack in the lower third of the oven. In a small saucepan, melt 1 cup of the butter and set it aside.

2 In the bowl of a stand mixer fitted with the whisk (or in a large bowl using a whisk), beat the eggs until they're frothy. Add the salt, brown sugar, date syrup, and vanilla and whisk until combined. Whisk in the melted butter. Using a spatula, fold in the teff flour until just combined. Fold in the almonds.

3 Remove the hot skillet from the oven and place the remaining 1 teaspoon butter in it. As it melts, brush the butter over the bottom and sides of the pan to coat. Pour half the batter into the pan. Scatter the halva over the surface of the poured batter, crumbling it with your fingers as you go. Pour the remaining batter over the halva, using a rubber spatula to smooth over the top.

4 Bake for 40 minutes, until the edges are darkening and beginning to crack and the middle is just set. You want the center to be barely cooked through, almost like warm cookie dough. Let it cool in the skillet for an hour. Then, using the Upside-Down Plate Trick (see page 56), flip it so it's right-side up. Cut it into 16 small wedges and serve.

CRISP TOFFEE BARS

makes 14 bars

1 cup (2 sticks) plus 1 teaspoon
unsalted butter

½ teaspoon salt

1 teaspoon vanilla extract

1 cup packed dark brown sugar

2 cups sifted unbleached all-
purpose flour

4 ounces (generous 1 cup)
slivered almonds, toasted

1 cup chocolate chips (use your
favorite brand/sweetness)

Maida Heatter's cookbooks have gotten a lot of mileage in my mom's kitchen. Whether she's covering soufflés or layer cakes, everything that meticulous doyenne of baking commands has a purpose. If she instructs you to line a cookie sheet with aluminum foil, it's to keep things like her Dolly's Crisp Toffee Bars—a frequent childhood request—from sticking. She promises "you will squeal with joy at the ease, fun, and satisfying excitement of peeling the foil from the smooth, shiny backs of the cookies." Yes! I know this squeal! I emit one every time I flip a finished bread or galette out of the cast-iron skillet and marvel at the ease with which the entire thing lands on the serving plate, not a trace of stuck dough left behind. This squeal is what justifies my oiling the pan after every use, or preheating it and adding butter to it before pouring in a batter, to be safe.

That is just what I do when, all these years later, I bake those same "chocolate chip butter bars," which are kind of like blondies in flavor and like crispy cookies in texture. If you make them in the skillet, as opposed to the shallower, wider jelly-roll pan Maida prescribed, they end up thicker, and you get a chewiness along with the crispy-crunchy.

The result is an improvement on something I thought couldn't get better. I didn't think I could like Maida Heatter any more than I already did, either, until I found out her "favorite pastime" was snacking in bed. Since then, I've decided it might be worth waking up with crumbs up my bum to bring one of Dolly's bars into my bedroom, with a glass of milk—to help me sleep, of course.

1   Preheat the oven to 350°F with a 10-inch cast-iron skillet placed on the middle rack.

2   In the bowl of a stand mixer fitted with a paddle, beat the 1 cup butter on low speed for about a minute, until it's softened. Scrape down the sides and base of the bowl, plus the paddle, as needed. With the mixer on low speed, add the salt and vanilla. Crumble in the brown sugar, then turn the speed up to medium and beat the mixture for 1 to 2 minutes, until it's the color of peanut butter and has aerated a bit. Stop the machine and scrape down the bowl again. Turn the mixer back on low speed and gradually add the flour, beating the mixture until it holds together. You may have to stop the machine to scrape the bowl again once or twice.

3   Add the almonds and chocolate chips and, using a wooden spoon, stir to combine them into the dough, which will be stiff.

4   Remove the hot skillet from the oven and place the remaining 1 teaspoon butter in it. As it melts, brush the butter over the bottom and sides of the pan to coat.

5   Using the wooden spoon, empty the dough into the skillet and, with your fingers, being careful to avoid touching the sides of the hot pan, press the dough to fill the skillet, evening it out as you go, until you have a solid, flat layer.

6   Bake for 30 to 35 minutes, until the top is a dark, golden brown. You may be tempted to take it out when the edges have begun to darken, but let it continue to cook so the entire surface can take on that color—you should start to see the dough bubble if you turn on the oven light and peer through the window.

7   Remove the skillet from the oven and let it sit for 1 minute before using a sharp knife to cut it into 14 bars. If necessary, run a butter knife around the sides of the pan to make sure the bars don't stick to the skillet. Let the bars cool completely before removing them. Use a small spatula or butter knife to transfer them to paper towels to blot the buttery bottoms. If you want to give them as a gift or save them for later, seal them, individually, in plastic wrap or wax paper; you can also place them in an airtight container. They should keep for up to 1 week.

8   Baked in advance, the dough would make a killer crust for an ice cream pie, too, and you should be able to remove it all in one piece rather than slicing it into bars, so you can layer the ice cream on top of it and transfer it to the freezer to set. Or else you could serve it in the skillet, cooled, without cutting it. Just plop on a few scoops of ice cream and drizzle some hot fudge over the top.

EXTRA-DARK ESPRESSO BROWNIES

makes 16 brownies

10 tablespoons plus 1 teaspoon
  unsalted butter

1¼ cups packed dark brown
  sugar

¾ cup plus 2 tablespoons best-
  quality unsweetened cocoa
  powder (preferably natural)

¼ teaspoon salt

3 tablespoons espresso powder,
  dissolved in 2 tablespoons hot
  water

½ teaspoon pure vanilla extract

2 large eggs, cold

½ cup rye flour

⅓ to ⅔ cup cacao nibs,
  depending on your preference
  (see Note)

Among many baking superpowers, Alice Medrich can claim seeing into the brownie's soul. Her thorough, ongoing investigation has yielded numerous recipes, none so famous as her New Classic Chocolate Brownies. The trick to these is to take perfectly undercooked brownies out of the hot oven and place the aluminum pan in an ice bath to stop them from cooking a second longer. But cast-iron isn't made for bathing. Plus, it holds more heat, and holds it longer than an aluminum pan; once you pull it out of the oven, your batter is going to continue to cook, and at a higher temperature. To avoid depressingly dry, stiff, sad blocks, you need to calibrate baking time and wetness accordingly.

I keep the skillet in the oven for the least possible amount of time required to yield actual brownies as opposed to hot, soupy batter. If you're struggling with the question of whether or not it's ready and wondering if just maybe you should put the skillet back in for a minute or two, you've nailed it. Stop, walk away from the pan, and leave your brownies to cool. When they do, they'll be perfect.

1   Preheat the oven to 325°F with a 10-inch cast-iron skillet placed on a rack in the lower third of the oven.

2   In a medium heatproof bowl set over a wide pan of gently simmering water (or using a double boiler), melt 10 tablespoons of the butter. Add the brown sugar, cocoa powder, and salt and cook, stirring from time to time, for about 7 minutes, until the mixture is smooth and almost hot enough to scald your finger. Remove the bowl from the heat. Let the mixture cool from hot to warm.

3   Add the espresso solution to the chocolate mixture and whisk to combine. Stir in the vanilla, then add the eggs one by one, whisking each one vigorously into the batter to aerate it before adding the next. Once the mixture is thoroughly blended, thick, and glossy, add the flour and stir until it completely disappears into the batter. Switch to a rubber spatula or wooden spoon and aggressively beat the batter for up to 60 strokes. Stir the cocoa nibs in, using more or less according to your preference and making sure they're evenly distributed.

4   Remove the hot skillet from the oven and place the remaining 1 teaspoon butter in it. As it melts, brush the butter over the bottom and sides of the pan to coat. Pour the batter into the skillet and bake for about 20 minutes, until the edges of the brownie have begun to pull away from the pan and a cake tester inserted into the center comes out wet with the sludge of batter. The interior should be gooey and almost seem underdone, the surface dry and shiny.

5   Let the brownies cool completely in the skillet, then cut them into wedges and serve them out of the pan.

> **NOTE**   These fudgy brownies are dark, skating dangerously close to bitter. If you're at all gun-shy about the bitter factor, you can use fewer nibs (⅓ cup, or less), but I like to push it to the maximum, and I appreciate the crunch.

ROSEMARY–OLIVE OIL BROWNIES WITH SEA SALT

makes 16 brownies

½ cup plus 1 tablespoon best-quality extra-virgin olive oil, plus 1 teaspoon

6 ounces bittersweet chocolate, coarsely chopped (see Note)

3 large eggs

¾ teaspoon flake sea salt

1 cup sugar

1 teaspoon vanilla extract

½ teaspoon almond extract

½ cup unbleached all-purpose flour

¼ cup almond flour

2 teaspoons orange zest

1 tablespoon finely chopped fresh rosemary

Fragrant with herbal, earthy, citrus, and nutty notes, this brownie is sweeter than the last and has a lighter consistency. Neither flourless nor cakey, its texture is like that of a flourless chocolate cake, with a soft, moist, pleasantly granular crumb. It also has a crackly, gleaming top, which its sibling does not. Three things account for that surface. The first is dark chocolate, which yields a shinier, shattering crust. The second is granulated sugar, which gives you the photogenic finish. The third is a good beating, which will also contribute to that luminous, crackled crown. You want to whip your eggs and sugar into a frenzy so they're at peak volume and pour out in a thick, glossy ribbon of pale yellow liquid. You'll need to get your stand mixer out for this. It makes a difference.

I combine the all-purpose with almond flour for added flavor and texture, and where others go infallibly classic with unsalted butter, I take a risk that pays off with a fruity extra-virgin olive oil. It imparts some moisture and a grassy-peppery aura. To complement that bouquet, I toss in rosemary. The element that prevents the herb and the olive oil from dominating the chocolate and delivering an unpleasantly savory brownie is the orange zest. The acid lifts those other ingredients. Sometimes, I find the combination of chocolate and citrus unsettling; in this recipe, I realize its potential. When these Mediterranean elements come together, they create a brownie different from any I've had before.

1 Preheat the oven to 350°F with a 10-inch cast-iron skillet placed on a rack in the lower third of the oven.

2 In a medium heatproof bowl set over a wide pan of gently simmering water (or using a double boiler), heat the ½ cup plus 1 tablespoon olive oil and the chocolate, stirring with a whisk, until the chocolate has melted and the mixture is smooth. Remove the bowl from the heat and set it aside.

3 Meanwhile, in the bowl of a stand mixer fitted with the whisk (or in a large bowl using a whisk), beat the eggs on high speed until they're frothy. Add ½ teaspoon of the salt, the sugar, and the vanilla and almond extracts and continue to whisk until the mixture is a thick and glossy pale yellow. Add the chocolate mixture and beat some more to incorporate. Using a rubber spatula, fold in the flours just until combined. Fold in the orange zest and rosemary.

4 Remove the hot skillet from the oven and place the remaining 1 teaspoon olive oil in it. Brush the olive oil over the bottom and sides of the pan to coat. Pour the batter into the skillet and sprinkle with the remaining ¼ teaspoon salt. Bake for 25 to 30 minutes, until the top is glossy and beginning to crack. The center should be just barely cooked—moist but set. Let it cool completely in the skillet before cutting it into 16 small wedges and serving them straight from the pan. These brownies are especially good the next day. You can cut the entire batch into wedges, wrap them tightly, and store them overnight.

> **NOTE** I'd go with a 62 to 68% chocolate, like Valrhona's Grand Cru Caraïbe 66%.

ON-THE-RISE BAKING

Opposite: The "Flying Duck" Pie, page 145

SWEET POTATO RUSKS WITH GARAM MASALA

makes about 30 rolls

1 medium sweet potato

⅛ teaspoon plus 1 teaspoon coconut oil, per batch

1¼ cups sorghum flour

5¾ cups unbleached all-purpose flour, plus at least ½ cup more for dusting and kneading

2¼ cups whole milk

2¼ teaspoons active dry yeast (one ¼-ounce packet)

2 teaspoons kosher salt

3 tablespoons coconut sugar

4 tablespoons (½ stick) unsalted butter, at room temperature

1 large egg

2 tablespoons garam masala

So-called rusks made of mashed potatoes were immortalized in the *New York Times* on April 29, 1887, and featured in Amanda Hesser's *The Essential New York Times Cookbook.* The rolls belonged to one "Aunt Addie," as she signed her recipe. But, as Amanda points out in the headnote for her book's version, "rusk" usually refers to stale country bread. These dried-out remnants served many purposes in the households of European peasants; they were used to give body to soups and stews, or offered as teething biscuits for babies, which is probably how we know them in this country. I repurposed Addie's recipe when developing this sweet-potato roll. I don't know what she would make of my adding an Indian spice blend, garam masala, to the dough. It's a mélange of aromatics that varies regionally but usually contains cinnamon, clove, cardamom, nutmeg, peppercorn, coriander, and cumin. Some of those are the same seasonings baked into Thanksgiving sweet potato pies. These "rusks," then, might not taste so exotic after all.

1 Preheat the oven to 375°F with a 10-inch cast-iron skillet in it. Place the sweet potato on a square of aluminum foil large enough to enclose it. Drizzle ⅛ teaspoon of the coconut oil on the sweet potato—just enough to coat—and rub the oil over the entire surface. Using a fork, prick the potato a few times, then wrap it in the foil; it should be well sealed, but not too tight. Place the potato in the skillet and roast for about 1 hour, or until a sharp knife stuck into the center glides through with little resistance and its interior is soft. It may need more time; check on it every 10 minutes until it's done.

2 Once the potato is cool enough to handle, peel it, discarding the skin, and, using a fork, mash the flesh in a small bowl. In a large bowl, whisk together the flours. In a separate large bowl, combine 1 cup of the potato, 2 cups of the milk, the yeast, and 3 cups of the flour blend and, using a wooden spoon, mix well. Cover the bowl and put it in a cool place for 2 to 3 hours, so the starter can

double in size. Alternatively, you can leave it in the fridge overnight.

3   Add the salt, 2 tablespoons plus 2 teaspoons of the coconut sugar, the butter, egg, garam masala, and 2½ cups more of the flour blend to the starter and, using a wooden spoon or rubber spatula, stir together until the dough is too stiff to stir any further. Turn it out onto a well-floured work surface and, dusting your hands with flour, knead it for about 10 minutes, until it's smooth and supple. It will start out quite sticky and you'll need to add more flour as you go—up to 2 cups. Add it in small increments, starting with ½ cup and decreasing, as you continue, to ¼ cup, ⅛ cup, and finally 1 tablespoon at a time. If you run out of the flour blend, use unbleached all-purpose flour. Once the dough has reached the desired texture, put it in a clean bowl, covered, for 1 to 1½ hours, until it's doubled in size.

4   Punch the dough down and turn it out onto a lightly floured work surface. Using a bench scraper or small sharp knife, slice pieces the size of large eggs and form them into balls, using your hand to form a dome over each as you gently press it in a circular motion against your work surface. Once you've shaped it into a loose bun, begin to speed up the circling, pressing motion until you've created a compact sphere. Place the rounds, smooth-side up, about ½ inch apart, on a flat surface lined with parchment paper, and cover them loosely. Let them proof for 30 minutes.

5   Meanwhile, preheat the oven to 400°F with a 10-inch cast-iron skillet in it. In a small bowl, dissolve the remaining 1 teaspoon coconut sugar in the remaining ¼ cup milk.

6   Remove the hot skillet from the oven and add 1 teaspoon coconut oil, tilting to coat. Fill the pan with 10 to 12 dough rounds, packing them close together. Choose the rounds in the order in which they were rolled. The remaining rounds can continue to proof while the first batch bakes.

7   Quickly brush the tops of the rounds in the hot skillet with the sweetened milk and bake for 20 minutes, until their tops have begun to brown, they're cooked through, and, if you tap on their bases, they sound hollow. During the baking process, they will likely become attached, but can easily be pulled apart for eating. Using a large spatula, you should be able to transfer them out of the pan in one go, as a loaf. Place them on a wire rack to cool while you cook the remaining rolls.

8   You will have enough for a complete second batch, and a few extra for a third; act quickly, baking one after the other so your dough doesn't overproof. For each, repeat the baking process, as above, adding 1 teaspoon of coconut oil to the hot skillet before placing the dough rounds in it and brushing them with the sweetened milk.

9   Leftover day-old or imperfect rusks can be used to make migas (see page 173), or toasted and spread with coconut butter and honey, mango chutney, or tomato jam.

NOTE In Pichet's original recipe, he calls for baking the pretzels "with steam until dark" to get a nice crust. I asked him what to do if, like me, you don't have a steam oven. "I just spray the walls of the oven, and/or put a pan of water at the bottom," he said. I tried the pan-of-water trick, and I'm sticking with it for this recipe. It's terrific.

CURRIED PRETZEL KNOTS

makes 10 knots

1½ teaspoons active dry yeast

⅓ cup plus 2 teaspoons warm
water (110° to 115°F)

3¼ cups bread flour, plus more
for dusting

½ teaspoon salt

2 tablespoons curry powder

1½ tablespoons vegetable or
canola oil, plus more for
greasing

⅓ cup plus 2 teaspoons
warm milk

¼ cup baking soda

1 large egg

1 teaspoon pretzel or other
coarse salt, or as needed

Curry Dipping Sauce (recipe
follows), for serving

Pretzel recipes aren't hard to come by, but I knew chef Pichet Ong's would be the benchmark, which it is, and that he would be open to my changing it, which he was.

I was in the market for something chubbier and tighter than the common cursive-shaped ballpark pretzels—something more like a knot that could be served with a meal, instead of biscuits or Parker House rolls, and that could be baked by the bunch. Their dough stained with curry powder, these stout, fragrant nuggets go in the oven in two shifts, five at a time. If you follow the directions and place the prepared dough in an alkaline bath of baking soda and water, you will get a true, golden pretzel crust. I encourage you to make my dipping sauce to accentuate the knots' aromatic side. The combination of mango chutney, honey mustard, and that Indian spice blend might sound weird to some; I think of it as a loosely interpreted, cheat version of *mostarda di frutta*—the Italian condiment of fruit conserves flavored with mustard seeds. I won't write you off if you don't try it; you'll be missing out, though.

1 In a small bowl, combine the yeast and warm water and let it rest for 10 minutes, until the yeast has dissolved and begun to foam.

2 Meanwhile, in a large bowl, stir together the flour, salt, and curry powder with a whisk. Add the oil, milk, and yeast mixture and, using a wooden spoon or rubber spatula, stir to combine. Pour ½ cup water over the mixture and use your hands to incorporate and form a tacky dough; it should be wet, but not sticky. If the dough is too dry, add more water, 1 to 2 tablespoons at a time, until you reach the desired consistency. Turn the dough out onto a lightly floured work surface and knead for up to 8 minutes, until it's pliant and smooth. Put the kneaded dough back in the bowl and cover it with plastic wrap or a kitchen towel. Let the dough rest for about 1 hour, until it has doubled in size.

3 While the dough is resting, in a small saucepan, bring 2 cups water to a boil. Remove from the heat and stir in the baking

(RECIPE CONTINUES)

soda until it has totally (or almost totally) dissolved. Set this alkaline solution aside to cool; it should be lukewarm, at most.

4   Meanwhile, preheat the oven to 450°F with a 10-inch cast-iron skillet placed on a rack in the top third of the oven.

5   Once the dough is ready, transfer it to a lightly greased Silpat baking mat or nonporous work surface. Using a bench scraper, divide the dough into 10 equal pieces. Shape them into logs, about 4 inches long, and let them rest, uncovered, for 5 minutes. Roll each log of dough into a thin rope 12 to 14 inches long and tie it into a chubby knot.

6   Pour the cooled alkaline solution into a 9-inch square pan. Place 5 of the pretzel knots in the pan, smooth-side down, and let them soak for 2 minutes. Flip them over and let their other sides soak for 2 minutes. Transfer the soaked knots to a large plate, allowing any excess solution to drain off of them as you lift them out of the pan, and let them sit, covered with a damp kitchen towel, for 10 minutes. Place the 5 unsoaked knots in the alkaline solution, giving each side a 2-minute soak. Transfer them to another large plate and cover them with a damp kitchen towel, too. (If you have a large enough kitchen towel, it can cover both plates.)

7   Empty the pan of the solution, give it a quick rinse, and fill it with fresh water. Place the pan on the bottom rack of the oven.

8   While the unbaked knots are proofing, in a small bowl, whisk the egg to incorporate the white and yolk, then whisk in 2 tablespoons of water to make an egg wash.

9   Once the first plate of knots has finished proofing, brush them liberally with the egg wash, then sprinkle them with ½ teaspoon of pretzel salt, adjusting to your preference.

10 Remove the hot skillet from the oven and place the 5 salted knots in it. Bake them for 10 minutes, until golden brown, rotating the pan halfway through. When the knots are almost done baking, quickly brush the 5 uncooked knots with the egg wash and sprinkle them with ½ teaspoon pretzel salt.

11 As soon as they come out of the oven, transfer the 5 baked pretzels to a large plate. Place the 5 unbaked knots in the hot skillet and bake for 10 minutes. Serve them, hot or warm, with the dipping sauce.

CURRY DIPPING SAUCE
makes approximately ½ cup

¼ cup mango chutney
¼ cup honey mustard
1 teaspoon curry powder
½ teaspoon salt, plus more to taste
½ teaspoon freshly ground black pepper, plus more
   to taste

In a small bowl, stir together all the ingredients. Taste for seasoning and adjust as needed.

WHOLE-WHEAT STICKY BUNS

makes 8 buns

DOUGH

¼ cup whole milk

4 large eggs

1¾ cups unbleached all-purpose
   flour, plus more for dusting

1⅓ cups whole-wheat flour

2 teaspoons active dry yeast

2 teaspoons fine sea salt

¼ cup plus 1 teaspoon
   granulated sugar

1 cup (2 sticks) plus
   3 tablespoons unsalted
   butter, well softened

FILLING

2 teaspoons ground cinnamon

2 tablespoons granulated sugar

TOPPING

¾ cup (1½ sticks) unsalted butter,
   well softened

½ cup plus ⅓ cup packed light
   brown sugar

¼ cup heavy cream

This thing looks as humble as any other old-fashioned homemade cinnamon roll, but when you sink your teeth into it, you become aware that Melissa Weller's bun is heads and shoulders above whatever Cinnabon or—sorry to the grandmas—mediocre heirloom you're used to. There are a couple of factors contributing to its superiority. One is whole-wheat flour. Somehow, when it's incorporated into a brioche dough and paired with a cinnamon-and-sugar filling, it lends only depth and a very subtle nuttiness—not a healthful-seeming trace to be found. Opting for *light* brown sugar in the butter topping is another thoughtful and beneficial decision. It complements that whole-wheat flour without overpowering it, and gives you the sticky bun's definitive caramelized goo without making the entirety taste like brown sugar. You can detect the sweet cream of the fat, and the earthiness of the spice, both of which *dark* brown sugar probably would have obscured.

1   **Make the dough:** In the bowl of a stand mixer fitted with the dough hook, combine the milk, eggs, flours, yeast, salt, and granulated sugar, in that order. Mix on low speed for 3 minutes, then raise the speed to medium and mix for 5 minutes more. Add the butter and mix on low for up to 8 minutes, until it is thoroughly incorporated into the dough, scraping down the sides and bottom of the bowl with a rubber spatula as needed. Remove the dough hook, cover the bowl with a kitchen towel, and let the dough rise at room temperature for 1 hour and 15 minutes.

2   Using a rubber spatula, scrape the dough out of the mixing bowl onto a parchment paper–lined baking sheet coated with nonstick cooking spray. Using your hands, gently coax the dough into a square shape, loosely cover it with plastic wrap, and refrigerate it until it's cold, about 1 hour.

(RECIPE CONTINUES)

3 **Meanwhile, make the filling:** In a small bowl, combine the cinnamon and granulated sugar and mix with a spoon until well combined.

4 Remove the dough from the refrigerator and transfer it to a Silpat mat or other flat work surface dusted liberally with flour. Using a floured rolling pin, roll the dough out to a rectangle that is 18 inches long by 12 inches wide. Roll it out horizontally, so the longer side is facing you.

5 Using a pastry brush, coat the entire surface of the dough with water. Sprinkle the cinnamon-sugar filling over the surface. Starting with the side closest to you, roll the dough up, jelly-roll style, to form a long log. Transfer the log, seam-side down, to a parchment paper–lined baking sheet, loosely cover it with plastic wrap, and place it in the freezer for 30 minutes, to firm it up for slicing (see Notes). If your freezer can't accommodate a tray large enough to hold the log, using your hands, adjust the shape of the log to fit a smaller tray or plate, making it shorter and thicker as needed.

6 **Meanwhile, prepare the topping:** In the bowl of a stand mixer fitted with the paddle, beat the butter and brown sugar together on low speed until just combined, scraping down the sides of the bowl as necessary. Add the cream and mix again to incorporate. (Do not overmix the topping; the less air you add, the better it bakes.) Spread the topping evenly across the bottom of a 10-inch cast-iron skillet.

7 Remove the log from the freezer and, using a bench scraper or sharp knife, slice it into 8 equal pieces and arrange them flat (i.e., cross-section style) in the skillet with one bun in the center and 7 circling it. (For the 2 end pieces, place the smooth, flat side in the topping, with the round sides sticking up.) Cover the skillet with a kitchen towel and leave the buns to proof for 2 hours.

8 Preheat the oven to 350°F, placing an aluminum foil–lined baking sheet on the lowest rack to catch any topping that bubbles up and out of the skillet during baking.

9 Transfer the skillet to the oven and bake the buns for 45 minutes, until light brown. Remove the skillet from the oven and let it rest for 5 minutes before carefully inverting the pan, using the Upside-Down Plate Trick (see page 56), and turning the sticky buns out onto a serving plate.

NOTES
- Cutting the sticky buns when the dough is super cold—almost half frozen—helps it keep its shape. Depending on your freezer, 30 minutes may not be enough time for your dough. Keep it in a few minutes longer, as necessary.

- Once filled and rolled, the dough log will keep for up to a week in the freezer. Thaw the frozen dough log for about 1 hour before slicing it and preparing it for baking. Make the topping while the dough thaws.

ENGLISH MUFFINS, MY WAY

makes 3 muffins

1 teaspoon active dry yeast

2 tablespoons plus 2 teaspoons
warm water (110° to 115°F)

2 tablespoons unsalted butter

¼ cup sour cream

¼ cup warm whole milk, steeped
with 1 star anise (see Notes)

½ tablespoon maple syrup

½ teaspoon salt

6 tablespoons graham flour

6 tablespoons unbleached
all-purpose flour

¼ cup quinoa flour, toasted
(see Notes)

½ teaspoon ground cinnamon

¼ teaspoon baking soda

Semolina, as needed, for
sprinkling the pan (see
page 94)

I always preferred Thomas' Cinnamon Raisin English Muffins to the Original variety—I only wished they'd removed the raisins. It's not that I don't like raisins, I do. A bowl of Raisin Bran hasn't lost its appeal, but in those breadstuffs, the dried grapes were getting in the way of my enjoying that soft, slightly sweet, warmly spiced dough. My second-choice Thomas' would be the Honey-Wheat. Whole-wheat flour is far from my favorite, yet somehow it works especially well in this instance. Must be the honey.

I kept all this in mind when dreaming up my ideal English muffin. I chose quinoa for my flour, but toasted it first. If you do that, you will get something wonderful out of it—a nuttiness that makes whole-wheat flour's seem pathetic. Maple syrup matched the quinoa's assertiveness, and I selected sour cream for a slightly more luxurious crumb. The volume on the spice needed to be raised to stand up to my other adjustments. Cinnamon alone wasn't enough. Star anise is a more complex, intense form of regular anise that has an

almost cinnamonlike note with a hint of black pepper. It gave my English muffins a depth that surpassed my ideal. Toast it, butter it, and anoint it with a swipe of apple or sweet potato butter.

1   In a small bowl, combine the yeast and the water and let it rest for about 5 minutes, until the yeast has dissolved and begun to foam.

2   In a 10-inch cast-iron skillet preheated over low heat or in a small saucepan, melt 1 tablespoon of the butter over low heat and pour it into a large bowl. Whisk in the sour cream, infused milk, maple syrup, salt, and the yeast mixture.

3   Add the flours, cinnamon, and baking soda and beat vigorously with a spoon or rubber spatula until thoroughly combined. Cover the bowl and let it rest in a warm spot for 1 to 1½ hours, or until the dough has doubled in size.

4 Preheat the oven to 350°F. Return the cast-iron skillet to the stove and preheat it, gradually increasing the heat from low to medium. When the pan is hot, add the remaining 1 tablespoon butter to melt, tilting to coat. When the butter is hot and sizzling, using a ½-cup measuring cup, drop one-third of the dough into the skillet to form a round muffin about 4 inches in diameter, mounding it slightly in the center. You may need to shape it a bit using your fingers; just be careful to avoid the hot edges of the pan. Repeat the process with the remaining two-thirds of the dough, until you have 3 muffins in the pan. Reduce the heat to low. Cover the skillet with a lid and cook the muffins for 3 to 5 minutes, until their bottoms are golden brown, making sure they don't burn.

5 Uncover the skillet and, using a spatula, flip the muffins. Cover the pan again and cook the muffins for 2 to 4 minutes, until the other sides are golden brown.

6 Turn off the heat and transfer the muffins to a plate. Wipe out any remaining butter in the skillet so it's dry and sprinkle its surface with a dusting of semolina. Put the muffins back in the pan, right-side up, and bake for 6 to 9 minutes, until they've finished puffing up and are cooked through. Split the muffins with a fork and toast before eating. You can also use them to make an NYC Rarebit Sandwich (page 186).

NOTES

- Quinoa flour has a sourish, grassy flavor and smell. In order to bring out its nuttier notes, you should toast it before adding it to any dough. To do so, heat a 10-inch cast-iron skillet over low heat. When the pan is hot, add the quinoa flour and, using a wooden spatula, stir continuously for about 5 minutes, until the flour has begun to take on a golden tone and has lost its grassy odor. Be careful not to burn it. Transfer the toasted flour to a small bowl and let it cool completely before using it.

- To steep the star anise, add it to a small saucepan with the milk and warm them together over low-medium heat to just below the boiling point. When you see little bubbles around the rim of the milk, remove the saucepan from the heat. To intensify the flavor, let the spice steep for 30 minutes (milder spices can go for up to 45 minutes or even 1 hour). This recipe calls for the spiced milk to be warm. If you've left it to sit and it has cooled, return the saucepan to the stovetop and warm the infusion gently over low heat. Discard the spice pod. You can try this technique with other whole spices. It applies to cream as well as milk; the higher the fat content of the liquid, the more intense the infusion.

DELHI BIALYS

makes 3 bialys

DOUGH

5 cups unbleached all-purpose
  flour

¼ teaspoon active dry yeast

2 teaspoons fine sea salt

1½ cups plus 1 tablespoon cool
  water (about 65°F)

Coarse whole-wheat flour
  (e.g., graham flour) or rye flour,
  for dusting

Onion Topping (recipe follows)

6 teaspoons bread crumbs

¾ teaspoon flake sea salt, plus
  more for finishing

SPICE MIX

2 tablespoons ghee or
  vegetable oil

1 teaspoon mustard seeds

1 teaspoon coriander seeds

1 teaspoon nigella seeds

1 teaspoon cumin seeds

1 teaspoon caraway seeds

9 curry leaves (fresh, preferably,
  but dried is okay)

Once sold at eastern European bakeries or delicatessens in Jewish neighborhoods like Manhattan's Lower East Side, bialys have become scarce. I grew up eating the round Polish bread whose dimpled center is topped with onions and, sometimes, poppy seeds, and was excited when New York City pastry chef and baker Melissa Weller told me she wanted to bring it back. She gave me her recipe for this book, but not before adapting it for a cast-iron skillet to yield a large, sharable bialy. Her instructions for kneading the dough were specific—she found that splitting it and putting each half in the food processor for a quick, intense spin, four times on and off, with one resting while the other whirls in the machine, results in the best-possible bialy a home kitchen can produce. She cooked down the onions—lots of them!—with great care, sweating them slowly on the stove at a low temperature before moving them to the oven and baking them, covered, for a half hour.

I did everything she instructed until, as my crispy, brown-crusted, chewy bialys cooled, I decided to leave off the poppy seeds. My brain had jumped from deli to Delhi, and I wanted to make a tempering—a fried blend of assorted spices used in Indian cuisine. I grabbed nigella, mustard, coriander, and cumin seeds from my spice cabinet and quickly toasted them in sizzling ghee until they popped and crackled. I threw in caraway seeds as well, to bring a hint of the Jewish bakery to my mix. At the last minute, I put some curry leaves in the pan. Then I spooned the hot aromatics and their golden cooking liquid over the bialys, letting the crunchy bits and unctuous fat settle into the onions.

(RECIPE CONTINUES)

1 **Make the dough:** In a large bowl, whisk together the all-purpose flour, yeast, and fine sea salt. Add the cool water and, using your hands, mix everything together until you don't see any flour.

2 Divide the dough in half. Transfer the first half to a food processor fitted with the dough blade and process for about 1 minute until the dough is warm—but not hot—to the touch. Set the first half aside and process the second half for about 1 minute. Repeat this procedure four times, waiting 1 to 2 minutes between kneadings to allow the food processor to cool down.

3 Transfer the kneaded dough halves back to the large bowl that you first used to mix the ingredients together. Cover it with plastic wrap or a kitchen towel and let the dough rest at room temperature for 1 hour and 15 minutes.

4 Give the dough a quick knead just to combine the halves, then, using a bench scraper, divide it into 3 equal pieces. Gently round each piece into a ball and set all 3 on a lightly oiled parchment paper–lined baking sheet. Cover the dough loosely with plastic wrap and refrigerate overnight or for at least 8 hours. (The dough will keep in the refrigerator for up to 3 days.)

5 Preheat the oven to 500°F with a 10-inch cast-iron skillet set on a rack in the middle of the oven. Heat the pan for a full 30 minutes.

6 Meanwhile, remove one of the pieces of dough from the refrigerator and let it warm up for 15 to 20 minutes. Dust your work surface with coarse whole-wheat flour and place the ball of dough on the dusted surface.

7 With your index and middle fingers, begin to punch down the dough, starting in the center of the ball and working out. Create a rim about 1 inch wide by dimpling the dough with your fingers. Stretch the dough by lifting it up from its center with your fist (just like you'd shape pizza dough). The stretched bialy should be 8 inches across. Spread ⅔ cup of the onion topping over the dimpled part of the bialy. Sprinkle 2 teaspoons of the bread crumbs and ¼ teaspoon of the flake sea salt on top.

8 Carefully pull the hot skillet out of the oven and place it on a heatproof surface. Using your hands or one hand and a large spatula, gently scoop underneath the bialy, trying not to disturb its topping. Quickly transfer it to the skillet and return the pan to the oven. Reduce the oven temperature to 450°F and bake for 15 to 20 minutes, until the crust is golden brown.

9   Remove the skillet from the oven and use a spatula to transfer the bialy to a wire rack. Repeat to make 2 additional bialys (see Note).

10 **Make the spice mix:** The 10-inch cast-iron skillet should still be hot from the oven. (If it isn't, preheat it, gradually raising the heat from low to medium-high.) Place it on the stovetop over medium-high heat and add the ghee. Once the ghee is hot, add the mustard and coriander seeds and fry them for about 1 minute, until they start to pop. Add the nigella, cumin, and caraway seeds and cook for 30 seconds. Add the curry leaves and cook for 15 to 30 seconds to wilt them.

11 Garnish each bialy with 1 tablespoon of the hot tempering and finish with additional flake salt, if desired. Feel free to eat them as is, or serve them with Roasted Eggplant Spread with Honey & Nigella (page 212).

> **NOTE** The second and third bialys can be made right away, or, as noted above, the dough can be kept in the refrigerator for up to 3 days.

ONION TOPPING
makes about 2⅓ cups

3 tablespoons unsalted butter
2 very large Spanish onions (about 2 pounds), thinly sliced
1 teaspoon fine sea salt

1 Preheat the oven to 300°F. Preheat a 10-inch cast-iron skillet on the stovetop, gradually raising the heat from low to medium. Once the pan is hot, melt the butter, then add the sliced onions and reduce the heat to medium-low. Cook for about 5 minutes, without stirring, so the onions start to shrink and become easier to move around the pan.

2 Cook the onions, stirring frequently, for 15 to 20 minutes more, until they are very soft and translucent and have not taken on any color. Stir in the salt, cover the pan with an ovenproof lid (cast iron, preferably), and place the onions in the oven to bake for 30 minutes.

3 Remove the onions from the oven, but do not lift the lid. Let the onions cool for 30 minutes without disturbing them. Uncover and drain the liquid from the onions. If not using immediately, store them in the refrigerator for up to 5 days. I like to prepare them the day before I need them.

CHICKEN LIVER & CIPOLLINI ONION PIZZA

makes four 8-inch pies

3 tablespoons unsalted butter

8 small cipollini onions, peeled and thinly sliced into rings (about 3 cups)

12 fresh sage leaves

½ teaspoon salt, plus more to taste

¼ teaspoon freshly ground black pepper, plus more to taste

½ pound chicken livers, sinew removed, minced

1 Pizza Dough (recipe follows)

1 cup grated Parmesan cheese

Extra-virgin olive oil, for drizzling (optional)

Aged balsamic vinegar, for drizzling (optional)

A couple of years ago, I changed my mind about chicken liver. Once I tasted a silky mousse and a pâté smooth as ganache on toast, I saw that it was capable of so much more than the mound of chopped mush my grandfather used to shove in my face and force me to eat. This recipe features a no-brainer ragout as a topping; it's gamy, earthy, savory, salty, and—because of those onions—a little bit sweet. I stuck with Jim Lahey's famous formula for no-knead dough, but I played with the dry ingredients, combining a bit of semolina flour with Italian "00". (The two zeros are used to indicate just how finely ground that flour is; it doesn't get finer.) With syrupy, aged balsamic vinegar and just-pressed olive oil drizzled on top, the first pizza had barely been polished off when I knew I needed a second. The good news was that one batch of dough makes enough for four pies.

1 Preheat the oven to 500°F. Preheat a 10-inch cast-iron skillet on the stovetop, gradually increasing the heat from low to medium-high. Once the pan is hot, melt the butter. Add the onions and sage and cook, stirring frequently with a wooden spatula, for 4 to 5 minutes, until lightly browned. Season the mixture with the salt and pepper, and stir again to combine. Add the chicken livers and cook for about 1 minute to sear them. Taste the mixture and adjust the seasoning accordingly. Transfer the mixture to a heatproof bowl and set it aside. It can be covered and kept in the refrigerator for up to 3 days, if you want to make it in advance or don't wish to cook all the pies at once.

2 While the cast-iron skillet is still hot, wipe it out and place it in the oven for 30 minutes to get extra hot. Switch the oven to broil for the next 10 minutes while you shape the dough.

3 Place one ball of dough on a well-floured work surface and dust it—and your hands—with more flour. Press the dough on the floured surface and, using the palms of your hands and your fingers to massage it, stretch it out into an 8-inch disc. Try to handle it as

little as possible. It's more than okay if you see a few gas bubbles in the dough; don't pop them. Alternatively, you can roll the dough out with a floured rolling pin. This will allow you to get a more perfect circle without any tears, though you will lose some of the desired blistering.

4   Remove the hot skillet from the oven and place the stretched dough in the pan. You should be able to pick up the dough with your hands and gently put it in the pan; you can also drape it over your rolling pin and then roll it into the pan. Working quickly, scatter one-quarter of the chopped liver topping over the dough, leaving a border of at least 1 inch. Sprinkle ¼ cup of the Parmesan over the topping. Put the skillet in the oven about 3 inches under the broiler and broil the pizza for 4½ minutes, or until the cheese is melted and golden and the crust has a nice char but isn't burnt. Using a spatula, transfer the finished pizza to a serving plate. Season it with salt and pepper, as needed. If you wish, drizzle your best-quality extra-virgin olive oil and, if you have it, some aged balsamic vinegar over it, too.

5   Repeat the process with the remaining dough and topping, keeping the broiler on and putting the skillet back in the oven while you stretch out the dough.

PIZZA DOUGH
makes 4 balls of dough

1 cup plus 2 tablespoons semolina flour
3 cups plus 3 tablespoons "00" flour
¼ teaspoon active dry yeast
2 teaspoons fine sea salt
Unbleached all-purpose flour, for shaping

1   In a large bowl, stir together the semolina and "00" flours, the yeast, and the salt using a whisk. Add 1½ cups water and, using a wooden spoon or your hands, combine thoroughly to form a dough. Cover the bowl with plastic wrap or a kitchen towel and leave it to rise at room temperature for 18 hours, or until it has more than doubled in size.

2   Liberally sprinkle unbleached all-purpose flour over your work surface and turn the dough out onto it. Using a bench scraper, divide the dough into 4 equal portions. Take one portion and pull each of its 4 sides out and around toward the center, beginning to form a ball. Use your hands to round it out and place it seam-side down, molding it into a tight sphere. If your dough ball is sticky, dust it with additional flour. Repeat the process with the remaining 3 pieces of dough.

3   If you're not planning to bake the dough right away, you can wrap each sphere separately in plastic wrap and store them in the refrigerator for up to 3 days. When you want to use the dough, bring it to room temperature 2 to 3 hours before you plan to bake it; just place it on your kitchen counter under a damp kitchen towel.

BIG SUR FOCACCIA

serves 8

1 cup warm water (110° to 115°F)

1 teaspoon active dry yeast

3¼ cups all-purpose flour

1 tablespoon plus 1 teaspoon fine sea salt

2 tablespoons sugar

½ cup extra-virgin olive oil, plus more for brushing

1 recipe Poolish (recipe follows)

½ cup cooked instant polenta, prepared according to the package instructions and cooled to warm or room temperature

Flake salt, for sprinkling

This focaccia is one of the best I've ever had. I attribute its excellence to Michelle Rizzolo of Big Sur Bakery. I've tried it plain and marveled at how good it is bare, with nothing on it, and how it can be used for everything from sandwiches to, when stale, panzanella (page 188), or even soup (page 184). I've also done it Rizzolo-style, with a layer of tomato sauce and Giardiniera (page 206) on top. Then, it's almost more like a pizza, and could be made a meal of.

A little instant polenta in the dough yields a moister, tastier focaccia. It's a small but brilliant improvement, and one I'd consider applying to other breads in the future.

1   In the bowl of a stand mixer fitted with the dough hook, mix the warm water and yeast on low speed to combine. Add the flour, salt, sugar, ¼ cup of the olive oil, and the poolish and mix for 2 minutes; the mixture should adhere and become thick and taffylike. Turn the machine off and crumble the cooked polenta into the bowl, making sure to break up any clumps. Turn the mixer up to medium

and mix for 4 minutes more. The finished dough should be smooth, shiny, and tacky. It will be relatively wet.

2   Pour the remaining ¼ cup olive oil directly into a 10-inch cast-iron skillet. Using a rubber spatula, turn the dough out of the bowl into the pan, gently rotating the dough in the oil until it's completely coated. Use your hands to spread the dough to fit the pan. Place the skillet in a warm area of the kitchen, cover it with a kitchen towel, and allow it to rise for about 90 minutes, or until it doubles in size. Press the dough gently with your fingertips to deflate it, then let it rise for 30 minutes more.

3   While the dough is proofing, preheat the oven to 425°F. Using your fingertips, press the dough down again, brush the top with more olive oil, and sprinkle it with flake salt.

(RECIPE CONTINUES)

4   Bake the focaccia for 20 minutes, then reduce the oven temperature to 375°F and bake for 15 to 20 minutes more, until golden brown. Let the focaccia sit in the pan for a couple of minutes before using the Upside-Down Plate Trick (see page 56) to flip it out, then transfer it to a wire rack, placing it right-side up. Slice it into 8 wedges and serve.

5   Leftover (1- to 2-day-old) focaccia can be used for pancotto (page 184) or panzanella (page 188). Store it in an airtight container at room temperature.

POOLISH

Any basic bread recipe can be adapted to contain a poolish, which deepens flavor. All it requires is pulling a tiny bit of yeast, water, and flour from the dough's ingredients, combining them, and letting the mixture sit overnight at room temperature. You can omit it from a recipe that calls for it: add the ingredients from the poolish back into the dough proper, mixing it in one go.

½ cup warm water (100°F)
¼ teaspoon active dry yeast
½ cup unbleached all-purpose flour

In a small bowl, using a wooden spoon or rubber spatula, mix the water, yeast, and flour to a thin paste. Cover the bowl with plastic wrap and leave it out overnight or for up to 15 hours at room temperature.

Focaccia Variations

Infuse the extra-virgin olive oil you use for brushing the dough with the chopped herb(s) of your choice by storing washed, dried, and gently bruised herbs with olive oil in a sealed bottle for 1 to 2 weeks away from sun and heat. Brush the mixture onto the surface of the dough before baking. The oil will prevent your herbs from burning in the oven.

Roast a head of garlic, squeeze out its cloves, and set them aside. When you press the focaccia dough down after the final 30-minute proofing, tuck the roasted garlic cloves into the resulting dimples. Brush the dough with extra-virgin olive oil, sprinkle with flake salt, and bake as directed.

Spread ½ cup tomato sauce over the top of the dough, followed by 2½ cups Giardiniera (page 206) drained of its oil. (If the vegetables in your giardiniera seem too dry, drizzle a tablespoon of that oil over them on the focaccia so they don't burn.) Sprinkle with a generous pinch of fine salt. Bake as directed, erring closer to 20 minutes for the second half of baking (at 375°F).

THE "FLYING DUCK" PIE

serves 4 to 6

FILLING

1 tablespoon duck fat

1½ cups large-diced onions

6 garlic cloves

1 celery stalk, thinly sliced

¾ teaspoon Chinese five-spice
powder

1 cup small-diced peeled potato
(russet ideally)

CHOUX

1 cup duck fat (you can use the
fat rendered when you make
Confit Duck Legs with Garlic)

1¾ cups bread flour

Pinch of salt

6 large eggs

3 cups thinly sliced green or
napa cabbage

1 Confit Duck Legs with Garlic
(recipe follows; see Notes)

1¼ cups (10 ounces) chicken or
duck stock

⅝ cup (5 ounces) English-style
pale ale

2 teaspoons soy sauce

¼ teaspoon Chinese five-spice
powder

Coarsely chopped fresh flat-leaf
parsley, for garnish

If ever you've wanted to wow your friends, this is
your golden opportunity. I started with a simple
premise: an updated English meat pie that, first
and foremost, could be baked in a cast-iron
skillet. What I had in mind was duck—its flesh
combined with East Asian flavors and its fat
used in the crust. I asked a legit Brit, pastry chef
Justin Gellatly of Bread Ahead bakery in London,
what he would do. What he suggested went well
beyond the limits of my imagination. Nestled
into a base of cabbage, the filling is comprised of
confitted duck legs and a garlicky potato-celery
hash that incorporates some of that slow-cooked
leg meat and is seasoned with Chinese five-spice,
a powder of Sichuan peppercorns, fennel seeds,
star anise, cloves, and cinnamon. A *pâte à choux*
dough—the stuff of éclairs and gougères—gets
piped around the whole thing, in little Hershey's
Kiss–shaped peaks. The completed masterpiece

looks like a mountain of licking flames with the
tips of four duck bones protruding—something
straight out of a *Game of Thrones* banquet.

This "mountain" appears much harder
to scale than it actually is. Each component,
including the pastry, can be made in the skillet,
on the stove. As the pie bakes, the choux blobs
balloon and, eventually, brown to form a proper
crust. What isn't as easy is piping it neatly and
uniformly. But no matter how rough or shoddy
your creation seems before you put it in the
oven, it will turn out better than you expected.

1   **Make the filling:** Preheat a 10-inch cast-iron
skillet on the stovetop, gradually increasing
the heat from low to medium. When the
pan is hot, add the duck fat and tilt to coat.
When the fat is hot, add the onions, garlic,

(RECIPE CONTINUES)

celery, and the five-spice powder. Sweat the vegetables for about 10 minutes, until they soften. Add the potato and sauté for 10 minutes or so more, until tender. Transfer the mixture to a medium bowl to cool.

2   **Make the choux:** In a 10-inch cast-iron skillet, combine 2 cups water and the duck fat and bring to a boil over medium-high heat. Remove from the heat and stir in the flour and salt to form a pastelike mixture. Put the pan back on the stove over medium heat and cook the paste for 2 to 3 minutes, stirring until it pulls away from the sides of the pan and starts to stick to the bottom. Remove from the heat and leave the paste to cool completely, at least 30 minutes.

3   Using a wooden spoon, beat in the eggs, one at a time, mixing each into the paste completely before adding the next one, until they're all incorporated and the mixture is glossy and smooth. Place the mixture in a bowl, cover with plastic wrap, and pop in the fridge for 1 hour.

4   **Assemble the pie:** Preheat the oven to 350°F. Place the cabbage on the bottom of the skillet. On top of that, layer the picked meat from the confit duck legs and the confit garlic. Nestle the 4 drumsticks in the pile of duck meat and cabbage, upside-down, so the bones are sticking up straight. Sprinkle the vegetable mix on top of the meat, working around the drumstick bones. In a small bowl, combine the stock, ale, and soy sauce, then pour the mixture into the skillet. Sprinkle the five-spice powder over the contents of the pan.

5   Remove the choux paste from the refrigerator and fill a large piping bag with it. You can either fit the bag with a ½-inch nozzle or else cut the tip of the bag at a 45-degree angle. Pipe ¾-inch rounds, giving them little peaks (so they look like little flames or Hershey's Kisses), all over the pie, going from the outside in, until the entire surface of the skillet is covered, with just the leg bones sticking out.

6   Bake the pie for about 90 minutes, until the pastry is golden brown and firm to the touch. Remove from the oven and garnish with the chopped parsley.

NOTES

• "Confit" is the word used to describe both the method for and outcome of preserving a food in fat. It involves salting the item, then slowly cooking it in fat until the meat browns and is fork-tender. Placed in a sealed container and covered with the strained, rendered fat, it will keep in the refrigerator for months.

• To prepare a confit duck leg that has been chilled, remove any excess fat that might have stuck to the meat. Place it skin-side down in a cast-iron skillet over medium-high heat and cook it for a few minutes, so the skin gets crispy and the rest warms through. You can order confitted duck legs and rendered duck fat. But you'd lose some of the flavor you get from following Justin's brining process, and, in turn, the fat rendered from the duck legs that were seasoned that way.

(RECIPE CONTINUES)

CONFIT DUCK LEGS WITH GARLIC
makes 4 duck legs

4 duck legs (about ½ pound each)

6 tablespoons coarse sea salt

12 whole black peppercorns

2 fresh bay leaves

1 head garlic, sliced in half

1 pound plus 1 tablespoon duck fat, plus
    2 teaspoons

1   In a deep tray or baking dish, place the duck legs in one layer. Sprinkle them with the salt, then rub them all over with it. Add the peppercorns, bay leaves, and garlic and rub those over the duck legs, too. Place the tray in the refrigerator and let the duck brine for 2 days.

2   When the duck legs are ready, take them out of the refrigerator. Remove the bay leaves and garlic and set them aside while you rinse the duck legs in cold water to remove all the salt. Place the duck legs in a bowl, cover them with fresh cold water, and soak them for 10 minutes. Rinse the duck legs again, place them back in the bowl with fresh cold water to cover, and soak them for another 10 minutes. Dry them with a kitchen towel or super-absorbent paper towel.

3   Set a 10-inch cast-iron skillet on the stovetop, place the duck legs, garlic, and bay leaves in it, and spread the duck fat over it. Cook over low heat for about 15 minutes, melting the fat so it covers the duck legs. Bring the fat to a gentle simmer, adjusting the heat as needed to maintain the simmer, and confit the legs for 3 to 4 hours, until the duck meat starts to give easily, almost falling off the bone.

4   Remove the skillet from the heat and let the duck begin to cool in the fat. Once the pan is no longer too hot to touch, strain the fat through a fine-mesh sieve, into a resealable container for later use. Leave the other contents in the skillet to continue cooling. Once the duck has reached room temperature, remove it from the pan and place it on a cutting board. Using a knife, separate the drumstick, bone intact, from the rest of each leg and, after removing its skin, set it aside. Remove all the meat from the rest of the duck legs and place it in a small bowl, discarding the skin and small bones. Squeeze the softened garlic cloves out of their skins and add the confitted garlic to the bowl. If any cloves have fallen out of the bulb during the cooking process, pick them out of the skillet and add them to the bowl, too. Discard the bay leaves and rinse and dry the skillet.

CHALLAH D'EPICES

makes 1 challah

DOUGH

3¼ cups unbleached bread flour,
   plus more for dusting

¼ cup rye flour

1¼ teaspoons ground cinnamon

1¼ teaspoons ground ginger

¼ teaspoon ground cardamom

¼ teaspoon ground white pepper

2 star anise pods, ground
   (¼ teaspoon to ⅜ teaspoon)

⅛ teaspoon freshly grated nutmeg

⅛ teaspoon ground cloves

3 tablespoons plus 1 teaspoon
   butter, plus softened butter for
   greasing

¾ cup warm water (110° to 115°F)

⅓ cup buckwheat honey

2 large eggs

3 large egg yolks

1 tablespoon finely grated
   orange zest

2 teaspoons active dry yeast

2 teaspoons coarse salt

GLAZE

4 tablespoons (½ stick) unsalted
   butter

¼ cup buckwheat honey

2 tablespoons plus 2 teaspoons
   fresh orange juice

1 star anise pod

¼ teaspoon ground cinnamon

¼ teaspoon ground ginger

One of the rituals for Rosh Hashanah, the Jewish New Year, is the eating of apples and honey to usher in a "sweet" year. Not long ago, I was hit with a sudden rush of filial devotion and thought I'd show up to my family's celebration of that event with a homemade challah that featured those auspicious ingredients. It was my first challah, and it was not baked in a cast-iron skillet. It made me proud, and it made my father, who gets extra solemn around the high holidays, happy. This is my second challah; it *is* baked in a cast-iron skillet. It makes me even prouder, and, possibly, my father less happy. Redolent with the flavors of a traditional *pain d'epices*—a French spice cake—it is the sort of thing that someone like me, who grew up celebrating both Hanukkah *and* Christmas, would come up with—a challah with a gingerbread soul.

1   **Make the dough:** In a large bowl, stir together the flours, cinnamon, ginger, cardamom, white pepper, star anise, nutmeg, and cloves with a whisk until well combined.

2   Grease a separate large bowl with butter to prevent the dough from sticking. In a small saucepan, melt 2 tablespoons of the butter and let it cool for a few minutes. Pour the melted butter into the greased bowl; add the flour mixture, warm water, honey, eggs, egg yolks, orange zest, yeast, and salt. Using a rubber spatula or wooden spoon, mix the ingredients until they come together into a dough. (As it gets harder to stir, you may want to work with your hands.)

(RECIPE CONTINUES)

3　Turn the dough out onto a floured surface and knead for 10 minutes, until the dough looks smooth and feels pliant. It will be relatively wet and sticky when you start kneading it, and you will probably need to continue to dust more flour onto your work surface as you go. Once the dough stops sticking to the surface, you will know it's ready.

4　In a small saucepan, melt 1 tablespoon of the butter over low heat and let it cool for a few minutes. Place the kneaded dough back in the greased bowl and brush the dough with the melted butter. Cover the bowl with a kitchen towel or plastic wrap, set it in a warm place, and let the dough rise for 90 minutes or until it doubles in volume.

5　Punch the down dough, cover it again, and let it rise and double in size again, giving it at least another 45 minutes. Meanwhile, in a 10-inch cast-iron skillet, melt the remaining 1 teaspoon butter over low heat. Remove from the heat and brush the melted butter over the bottom and sides of the pan to coat.

6　Turn the dough out onto a lightly floured surface and, using a bench scraper or sharp knife, split it evenly into halves. With both hands, roll one half out into a thick, foot-long rope. Do the same with the second half. Coil the first rope into a circle and put it in the center of the buttered skillet. Then wrap the second rope around the first, tucking the edges of the outer rope under

those of the inner coil to connect the 2 ropes (see photographs on page 154).

7　Butter a piece of plastic wrap and cover the dough in the pan. Let it rise one more time for about 45 minutes. Meanwhile, preheat the oven to 375°F with a rack placed in the lower third of the oven.

8　**Make the glaze:** In a small saucepan, combine the butter, honey, orange juice, and star anise pod and bring to a simmer over medium-low heat. Remove from the heat and stir in the cinnamon and ginger. Let the glaze cool in the saucepan for a few minutes, leaving the star anise to steep. Brush the dough liberally with the glaze (about 2 tablespoons), reserving the rest.

9　Bake the bread until it is golden brown and sounds hollow when you knock on it (the true test of whether a challah is cooked or not), about 35 minutes. As soon as the challah comes out from the oven, brush it with another liberal coating of the glaze (about 2 tablespoons). Leave it in the skillet for a couple of minutes to set before transferring the challah to a wire rack to cool for about 30 minutes. You should be able to lift it out of the pan quite easily with a spatula.

10　Reserve any remaining glaze and leftover, stale challah to make Gingerbread Challah Bostock (page 179).

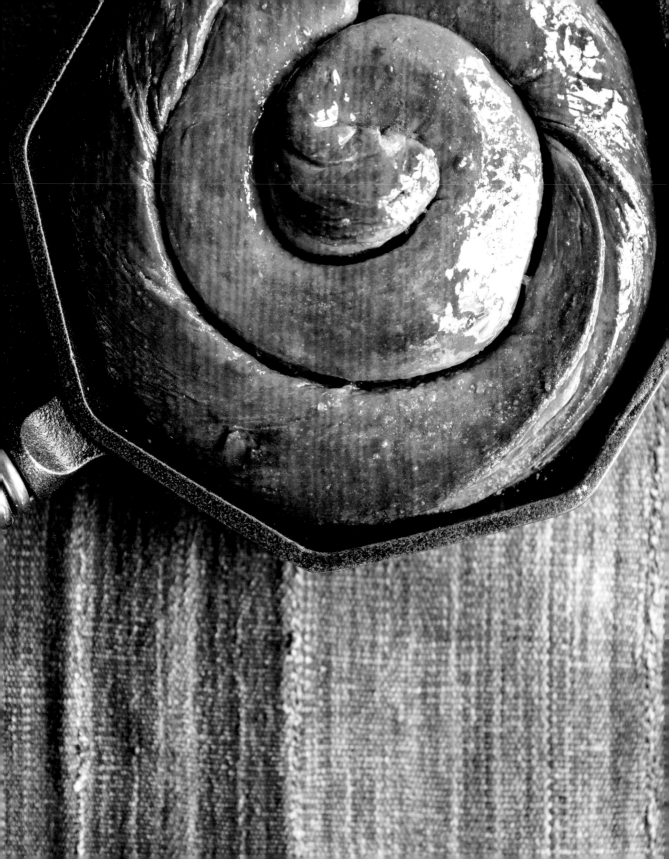

PISTACHIO-CHERRY DANISH

makes 1 large Danish

DOUGH

¾ cup whole milk

1 vanilla bean

¼ cup warm water (110° to 115°F)

2¼ teaspoons active dry yeast
(one ¼-ounce packet)

½ cup sugar

1 teaspoon salt

2 large eggs

5 to 5½ cups sifted unbleached
all-purpose flour

¼ teaspoon ground cardamom

8 tablespoons (1 stick) unsalted
butter, at room temperature

FILLING

⅔ cup dried cherries

¼ cup dark rum or other dark
liquor

2 egg whites

¾ cup packed pistachio paste

2 tablespoons sugar

4 tablespoons (½ stick) unsalted
butter, at room temperature

Zest of 1 lemon

1 teaspoon unsalted butter

1 egg yolk, for the egg wash

¼ cup coarsely chopped
pistachios, for sprinkling

1 teaspoon sugar, for sprinkling

⅛ teaspoon salt, for sprinkling

New Year's Eve is a holiday I have little patience for and barely celebrate. I have two methods of coping: either leaving the country for someplace that isn't teeming with tourists and *Best Night Ever!* cavorters, or staying home in my pajamas, drinking champagne, and eating something outrageously luxurious while watching old movies. A few years ago I was going with Option 2 and hadn't figured out what my lavish culinary indulgence would be. Then I read something Amanda Hesser wrote about her mother's Danish, and I became dead set on perfecting my own. There was no kneading required, and I just had to proof the dough overnight in the fridge. Filling and twisting it was just as painless. It was so good, I didn't bother to let it cool and wait for the stupid ball to drop. I stood in my kitchen, ignoring everything else, as I stuck my fork in a slice, repeatedly, before cutting a second, larger piece.

Later, when I got the idea of using pistachio paste in the filling, I knew I was going to see fireworks. Cherry and pistachio are a pastry power couple; theirs is a lusty, electric love for the ages. That first taste of Danish is like one of those Crash Davis–style "long, slow, deep, soft, wet kisses that last three days." And now December 31 can't come soon enough.

1 **Make the dough:** Place the milk in a small saucepan. Split the vanilla bean in half and scrape the seeds out into the saucepan. Add the scraped, split pod to the pan, too. Warm the milk over medium heat, bringing it just under a boil. When you see little bubbles around the rim and the milk is steaming, remove the pan from the heat and let the milk cool to lukewarm.

(RECIPE CONTINUES)

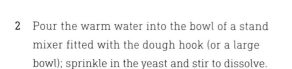

2   Pour the warm water into the bowl of a stand mixer fitted with the dough hook (or a large bowl); sprinkle in the yeast and stir to dissolve.

3   Add the lukewarm milk, sugar, salt, eggs, 1 cup of the flour, and the cardamom and mix together on low speed. Add the butter and mix to combine. Beat in 2 cups of the flour until the mixture is smooth. Add enough of the remaining flour to form a supersoft dough.

Knead it in the mixer with the dough hook, or turn it out onto a work surface dusted with flour and knead it by hand for 3 to 4 minutes, until the dough is supple and silky smooth and small blisters develop just under its surface. Put the dough in a large well-greased bowl, turning the dough over so it's greased-side up. Cover the bowl with plastic wrap and refrigerate overnight.

4   The next day, take the dough out of the refrigerator and punch it down. Transfer it from the bowl to your countertop and cover it with a kitchen towel. Let it rise a second time, at room temperature, for up to 90 minutes, or until almost doubled in size.

5   **While the dough rises, make the filling:** In a small saucepan, combine the cherries, rum, and ¼ cup water. Bring the mixture to a simmer, cook it for 2 minutes, then remove it from the heat and let it cool. Drain the liquid from the mixture and set the cherries aside in a small bowl.

6   In a food processor, pulse the egg whites until they're foamy. Crumble in the pistachio paste and pulse again until it's thoroughly combined and smooth. Add the sugar and butter and pulse again to incorporate. Using a rubber spatula, scoop the mixture into a medium bowl. Add the lemon zest and stir to combine.

7   **Assemble the Danish:** Preheat the oven to 350°F. Line a baking sheet with parchment paper. In a 10-inch cast-iron skillet, melt 1 teaspoon butter over low heat. Brush the melted butter over the bottom and sides of the pan to coat.

8   Turn the dough out onto a lightly floured work surface. Cut it into 4 equal pieces; you will be making 2 twists. Roll each piece out to a 5 by 12-inch rectangle. Using a rubber spatula or the back of a spoon, spread one-quarter of the pistachio paste mixture on each rectangle; dot each with one-quarter

of the drained cherries. Roll each piece up from the long side, jelly-roll style. Pinch the edges and ends well to seal the seams and help keep the filling inside the dough. Place 2 of the filled rolls side-by-side, seams down. Twist one roll over the other, as tautly as possible, forming a thick rope. Pinch the ends of the twist to fuse the rolls together, and tuck or twist any less-than-pretty areas under, out of view. Repeat with the remaining rolls.

9   Coil the first twisted rope into a small, tight, snaillike spiral circle and place it in the center of the skillet. Wrap the second twisted rope around it, tucking the edges under the inner coil to connect the two ropes.

10 Beat the egg yolk with 2 tablespoons water to make an egg wash and brush the dough with it. Sprinkle the pistachios over the top, followed by the sugar and the salt. Cover the pan and let the dough rise once more until doubled in size, about 40 minutes.

11 Bake the Danish until it's browned and cooked through, 30 to 35 minutes, rotating the pan 180 degrees halfway through. Remove it from the oven, leaving it in the skillet for a couple of minutes to set before transferring it to a wire rack to cool for about 30 minutes. You should be able to lift it out of the pan quite easily with a spatula. This is best eaten the same day it's baked. I don't even let mine cool; it's a bit messier, but I can't help myself.

CORNFLAKES-N-MILK CAKE

serves 4 to 6

BATTER

1½ cups cornflakes

1½ cups cold whole milk

3 large eggs

1½ cups sugar

6 tablespoons (¾ stick) plus
   2 teaspoons unsalted butter

1½ cups unbleached all-purpose
   flour

½ teaspoon salt

1½ teaspoons baking powder

1 teaspoon vanilla extract

CORNFLAKE GANACHE

3⅔ cups cornflakes

1⅓ cups heavy cream

10 ounces Valrhona Dulcey Blond
   Chocolate, finely chopped

1½ tablespoons unsalted butter,
   cut into 3 pieces and softened

⅜ teaspoon salt

While you'd typically make a layer cake using "normal" circular aluminum baking pans, isn't it nice to know you don't need them? That you can do it with a single cast-iron skillet? A tribute to baker Liz Lorber in Atlanta, who introduced me to Hot Milk Cake and got my wheels turning, this recipe also reminds me of my father. He's almost always on a diet, and whichever one it is, it usually forbids cereal. Sometimes he'll say, with such longing, that all he wants is a simple bowl of cornflakes and milk—or even better, cornflakes and *cream*. Poor Dad! If only he wasn't on a diet, again, I'd cut him a square of this crunchy-coated, fluffy cake.

1 **Make the batter:** Preheat a 10-inch cast-iron skillet on the stovetop, gradually raising the heat from low to medium. When the pan is hot, add the cornflakes and toast for about 6 minutes, shaking the pan frequently and vigorously, and watching to make sure they don't burn. Transfer the cereal to a 5½-inch strainer.

2 Place the strainer with the toasted cornflakes in a small saucepan. Pour the cold milk over the strainer into the saucepan, so that the cereal is immersed in the milk. Cover and warm the milk over medium-low heat. Bring the mixture just below its boiling point; when you see little bubbles around the rim of the milk, remove it from the heat (this should take up to 10 minutes, but you should check your milk at 7 or 8 minutes, to be safe). Let the mixture sit, covered, for 45 minutes.

3 While the cornflakes are steeping in the milk, preheat the oven to 350°F with a 10-inch cast-iron skillet in it.

4 In the bowl of a stand mixer fitted with the whisk, beat the eggs until foamy, starting on medium-low and increasing the speed as you go. Whisk the sugar in gradually and continue beating until the mixture is thick and glossy.

5 Remove the strainer from the milk and discard the cornflakes. Measure out ¾ cup of the infused milk and discard the remainder. Return the reserved milk to the saucepan and add the 6 tablespoons butter. Cook over medium heat, stirring, until the butter melts.

6 In another bowl, sift together the flour, salt, and baking powder. Using a rubber spatula, fold the dry ingredients into the egg-sugar mixture. Add the buttery milk all at once and stir just to combine. Add the vanilla and stir again to incorporate.

7 Remove the heated skillet from the oven and add 1 teaspoon of the butter, letting it melt and brushing it to coat the bottom and sides. Pour half the batter (2 cups) into the prepared pan. Bake for 25 minutes, or until just done, when the top is golden brown and the edges are crispy. Insert a cake tester and it should come out clean. You're looking for a moist crumb. Leave the cake in the skillet for 2 minutes before using a spatula to loosen it from the sides of the pan. Get under it with the spatula to make sure it isn't sticking to the bottom of the skillet. Using the Upside-Down Plate Trick (see page 56), flip the cake out, then transfer it to a wire rack, placing it down right-side up. Make sure the skillet is free of cake residue, then immediately melt the remaining 1 teaspoon butter in the hot pan, as before, brushing to coat. Pour the remaining batter into the skillet and bake as you did the first cake. Follow the same instructions as above, leaving the second cake on a wire rack so it can cool.

8 **Meanwhile, make the cornflake ganache:** Toast 1⅓ cups of the cornflakes as above. Place the toasted cornflakes in a 5½-inch strainer and set it in a small saucepan. Pour

(RECIPE CONTINUES)

the cold cream over the strainer into the saucepan, and warm and steep, following instructions in step 2.

9 Remove the strainer from the cream and discard the cornflakes. Measure out ⅔ cup of the infused cream and discard the remainder. Return the reserved cream to the saucepan and bring it to a boil over medium-high heat.

10 Place the chocolate in a medium heatproof bowl. Pour the boiling cream over the chocolate and let it sit for 30 seconds. Using a rubber spatula or whisk, gently stir the cream and chocolate together, first making small circles in the center of the bowl, and then, as the ingredients begin to blend, widening the radius of the circles to incorporate the entire bowlful of cream and chocolate. Once you have a smooth ganache, stir in the butter, one piece at a time, just to combine. It should look like a shiny caramel glaze. Add the salt and stir to combine. Let the ganache rest at room temperature to thicken up so that it's still pourable and easy to spread.

11 Meanwhile, toast the remaining 2⅓ cups cornflakes as above. Transfer the toasted cornflakes to a bowl and set aside.

12 When both cakes have cooled completely, slice off the round edges of each to yield two 6-inch square layers. (I cut them while they are resting on the wire racks.) Save the scraps for a snack (see Note).

13 On a cake stand or raised plate, place the first 6-inch square layer of cake. Pour ¼ cup of the ganache onto the center of the layer and, using an offset (cake) spatula, spread it over the surface. Add another ¼-cup scoop of ganache and continue to spread it, coating the entire layer so you can't see the cake beneath it. If you prefer a thicker center seam of ganache, you can add another tablespoon or two, or even a third scoopful. Don't worry if some spills over the edge.

14 Place the second cake layer on top of the first and frost as above. Spread the spillover around the sides of the layered cube using your offset spatula to dip into and pick up more ganache from the bowl, as needed, smoothing the frosting as you go. Catch any ganache puddles with the spatula and use them to finish coating the sides evenly.

15 Once the entire surface of the cube is coated in a smoothed layer of ganache, use your hands to cover the entire exterior of the cake with the remaining toasted cornflakes, gently patting them on; they should readily adhere to the ganache.

16 Use a damp kitchen towel or paper towel to clean up any drippings on the cake stand, carefully blotting around the perimeter of the cake. Present it, as is, bringing it to the table and slicing it to serve. It should be eaten the same day it's made, and it's a small cake, so you don't have to worry about having leftovers.

NOTE Cake baked in a skillet is slightly sloping, so this recipe calls for trimming the edges of the rounds to turn them into squares, for a cube-shaped result. As I worked on this recipe, I wanted to do something special with those scraps. So, I cubed them and put them in a bowl with heavy cream, extra cornflakes, and a sprinkle of salt. Voilà—a baker's snack.

SKILLET PANCAKE SOUFFLÉ

serves 4 to 6

1 cup unbleached all-purpose
  flour
1 teaspoon baking powder
2¾ cups buttermilk
½ teaspoon salt
3 tablespoons unsalted butter

⅓ cup plus ½ teaspoon sour
  cream
½ teaspoon vanilla extract
1 tablespoon Grand Marnier
4 large egg yolks (see Notes)
5 large egg whites (see Notes)

⅛ teaspoon cream of tartar
¼ cup plus 1 tablespoon
  granulated sugar
Confectioners' sugar, for dusting
Orange–Maple Syrup Sauce
  (recipe follows), for serving

Chef Pichet Ong was so excited about this cast-iron baking project that he offered me a prized recipe as a gift. This pancake-flavored soufflé—a billowing, golden-rimmed vision, rising out of a skillet—is unbelievable. Dutch baby pancakes never get so tall, and whatever height they have deflates before you can pull them out of the oven. Pichet managed to create something with a cloudlike interior that, even in a wide pan, could swell and hold its shape. It is barely sweet, so you can sauce or sprinkle it according to your mood. Coat the top with confectioners' sugar, spoon it onto a plate with a few dollops of raspberry jam or orange marmalade, perhaps, and dig right in. If you want to play up the pancake factor and bring some old-fashioned fine dining to the experience, serve it in its skillet tableside, pouring a warm, Grand Marnier–spiked maple-syrup sauce and some fresh berries into the center of the soufflé. Or, for less drama and more practicality, I leave the sauce in a pitcher, so people can drizzle it over as generously as they like.

1 Sift the flour and baking powder together into a medium bowl.

2 In a large, high-sided saucepan, stir together the buttermilk and salt. Add 2½ tablespoons of the butter and bring the mixture to the brink of boiling over medium-high heat (you should see smoke coming off the surface and lots of frothy bubbling action around the edges). Stir it occasionally to incorporate the melting butter. Using a whisk, add the flour mixture and cook for about 1 minute, until a smooth paste forms, whisking vigorously and continuously to avoid having too many lumps. Remove it from the heat.

3 Add the sour cream, vanilla, and Grand Marnier and whisk aggressively to combine. Vigorously whisk the egg yolks into the mixture, making sure to incorporate them thoroughly. Transfer the batter to a large bowl to cool down a bit; it should remain warm.

(RECIPE CONTINUES)

4   Preheat the oven to 350°F with a 10-inch cast-iron skillet placed on a rack in the middle of the oven.

5   In the bowl of a stand mixer fitted with the whisk (or in a medium stainless steel or copper bowl using a whisk), beat the egg whites and the cream of tartar on medium speed for 2 minutes, until the whites are frothy. Gradually add ¼ cup of the granulated sugar and continue to whip for another 3 to 4 minutes, until the whites hold medium peaks.

6   Fold half the meringue into the batter to lighten it up. Once the first half of meringue is fully incorporated, fold in the remaining half.

7   Remove the hot skillet from the oven and add the remaining ½ tablespoon butter. Once the butter has melted, brush it over the bottom and sides of the skillet to coat. Sprinkle the base of the skillet with the remaining 1 tablespoon granulated sugar. Pour the batter into the prepared pan, using an offset spatula to smooth out and even off the top. Bake for about 25 minutes, until the top is dry, the edges are beginning to brown, and the pancake rises to about twice the height of the batter. Do not disturb your soufflé while it's baking; leave the oven door shut!

8   Serve the hot soufflé in the skillet. Dust it with confectioners' sugar (about 1 tablespoon) and serve it with the warm Orange–Maple Syrup Sauce on the side.

NOTES
- Eggs are best separated cold, but for maximum volume, egg whites are best beaten into meringue at room temperature. Get your yolks and whites sorted ahead of time, then let them come to room temperature before starting the rest of the recipe.

- This batter can be made ahead of time and refrigerated overnight.

ORANGE–MAPLE SYRUP SAUCE
makes about ¾ cup

¾ cup maple syrup
1 tablespoon Grand Marnier
Zest of ½ orange
1 tablespoon butter
¼ teaspoon salt
½ cup fresh raspberries and/or blueberries

1   In a small saucepan, cook the maple syrup over medium heat for 6 to 8 minutes, reducing it in volume, until the first sign of smoke.

2   Remove the pan from the heat, add the Grand Marnier, orange zest, butter, and salt and whisk together, just until the butter has melted and all the ingredients are incorporated. Add the berries, giving them a quick, gentle stir with a wooden spoon to combine.

WHOLESOME APPLE-QUINCE PIE

serves 10 to 12

FILLING

2 medium quince

Juice of 1 orange

1½ cups white wine

2⅔ pounds apples

1 vanilla bean, split lengthwise
   and seeds scraped

⅛ teaspoon flake sea salt

12 pink peppercorns, finely
   ground

½ teaspoon orange zest

⅔ cup sugar

CRUST

2 cups spelt flour

½ cup unbleached all-purpose
   flour, plus more for dusting

¾ cup (1½ sticks) unsalted butter,
   cut into ¼-inch cubes and
   chilled (see Notes)

6 tablespoons ice water, or as
   needed

1 large egg

2 tablespoons sugar

½ teaspoon sea salt

I love Heather Lanier's approach to pie. As the owner of the farm, wellness retreat, and cooking school Hill of the Hawk in Big Sur, she makes pies that are stripped down so you can taste each ingredient, highlighting the fruit, which, lucky her, comes straight off the trees a few feet away from the counter where she rolls out her dough. Every note of Heather's recipe—apple, quince, spelt, and butter—strikes clearer, louder.

The crust is as easy as you-know-what. It's all done by hand, in a matter of moments, while the apples and quince are macerating in their spices and some sugar. Best of all, you don't even need to stop to chill the dough. Straight into the oven it goes and an hour later, it's ready. Pure pie, that's what it tastes like.

1 **Make the filling:** Quarter the quince. Core and peel them, then halve each quarter so you end up with 8 slices per quince. In a medium skillet or wide saucepan, cover the quince with the orange juice and wine. Cover and bring the liquid to a simmer over medium heat. Cook for about 35 minutes, until the liquid takes on a rose tint and the fruit's flesh is soft enough to pierce with a knife.

2 While the quince simmer, peel and quarter the apples, then thinly slice them, about ⅛ inch thick. Set them aside in a large bowl. In a small bowl, stir together the vanilla seeds, salt, pink peppercorns, and orange zest.

3 Drain the quince and transfer the fruit to a cutting board to cool. Slice the quince a bit thicker than the apples (about ¼ inch thick) and add them to the bowl with the apples. Using your hands or a wooden spoon, toss the apples and quince together to combine. Sprinkle the sugar over the fruit and toss

(RECIPE CONTINUES)

again to coat it evenly. Pour the spice mixture over the fruit and toss again to incorporate.

4 **Make the crust:** Preheat the oven to 350°F. In a large bowl, whisk together the flours. Add the butter and, using your fingers, rub it into the flour, breaking it down into pea-size pieces so you have what resembles a coarse meal. Dribble 3 tablespoons of the ice water over it and, using your hands, stir to incorporate the liquid so you begin to form a dough. Continue to add more water, 1 tablespoon at a time, just until the dough comes together; it shouldn't be too crumbly or dry. You may need to add up to 3 tablespoons more, but be careful that the dough doesn't become too wet or sticky.

5 Cut the dough into equal halves and shape each into a ball with your hands. Flatten both balls into discs and place them on a floured work surface.

6 Place a 10-inch cast-iron skillet and the bowl of apple-quince filling as close to your rolling station as possible. Roll the first disc of dough out into a circle 11 to 12 inches in diameter, rotating it 45 degrees after every few rolls, and flipping it over once or twice to get an even thickness. Use a bench scraper or a long spatula to gently peel the dough away from the work surface so you can lift it, carefully, into the skillet. Push the excess dough up around the edges of the pan. Repeat with the other disc of dough, setting it aside while you pile the fruit into the pan.

7 Pour off any extra juice that has pooled at the bottom of the bowl of fruit. Using a

slotted spoon, place the filling in the dough-lined skillet, patting the fruit down to make sure it's lying flat. Carefully lift the second dough circle and place it on top of the filling. Fold down the excess dough toward the outside of the skillet, then crimp it in a fun shape around the entire edge.

8 In a small bowl, beat the egg with ¼ teaspoon water to make an egg wash. Brush the entire surface of the top crust with the egg wash, giving it a thick coating.

9 In another small bowl, mix the sugar with the salt together to combine, and sprinkle the mixture over the top crust. Using a sharp knife, make two small, clean incisions to form a cross, so steam can escape. Bake for 1 hour, until the crust is golden and the edges are browned. Let the finished pie cool for at least 45 minutes before slicing into it and serving it straight out of the skillet.

NOTES

- Make sure to dice the butter into smaller cubes than you might for other crusts, because you will not be chilling the dough before baking it. Move quickly to incorporate the butter into the flour so it stays chilled and doesn't begin to melt. The finer the dice, the faster you can work.

- Feel free to fancy or fatten this pie to your taste: cover the fruit in spiced, salted, or plain-old caramel sauce, or top each slice with a piece of good-quality sharp cheddar.

MAKE-THE-MOST-OF BAKING

Opposite: Migas with Sweet Potato Rusks & Chinese Sausage, page 173

EXTRA-COCONUTTY EGGS-IN-A-HOLE

makes up to 4 large rotis

4 tablespoons coconut oil

1 recipe Extra-Coconutty Roti batter (see page 27)

4 large eggs

4 teaspoons coconut butter

4 tablespoons maple syrup

6 teaspoons dark soy sauce (see Notes)

6 tablespoons unsweetened coconut flakes, toasted (see Notes)

For someone who is more interested in eating than cooking, my father's breakfast game is strong. When my brother and I were little, one of our favorites was what Dad did with a piece of bread, a lot of butter, an egg, and a slice of American cheese. It was a Sunday treat, made when Mom was sitting under her egg-shaped hair dryer and we couldn't contain our hunger anymore. "Egg-in-a-hole with cheese, please!" we'd shout.

This recipe introduces my roti to the flavors of a Singapore specialty called *kaya* toast, which is filled with butter and a sweet coconut jam and dipped into soy sauce–seasoned soft-boiled eggs. I cut a hole in the roti's center, flip it over, and, just like Dad did, place an egg in the well. When it's ready, I smear it with coconut butter and drizzle it with maple syrup and soy sauce. For this "egg-in-a-hole," skip the cheese, please, and thank you.

1   Preheat a 10-inch cast-iron skillet on the stovetop, gradually raising the heat from low to medium. Once the pan is hot, add 2 teaspoons of the coconut oil and tilt to coat. Drop 1 cup of roti batter into the pan. In the first minute, use a spatula to flatten and spread the batter—it should be ¼ inch thick and take up most of the skillet, leaving some room for flipping—and then use a 2½-inch biscuit cutter to remove a hole in the center of the cooking roti. Leave the roti to cook for 3 minutes more, until its underside begins to brown, then flip it over with a spatula.

2   Quickly reduce the heat to medium-low and add 1 teaspoon of the coconut oil into the hole in the roti. Crack an egg into the hole. Cook for 2 minutes, then cover the pan for another minute, until the egg whites have just set but the yolk is still runny. If the egg whites haven't quite set, continue cooking the roti, uncovered, until they have, watching the pan very closely so the egg doesn't overcook.

3   Immediately take the pan off the heat and, using a spatula, move the egg-filled roti to a serving plate. Spread 1 teaspoon coconut butter on it; drizzle it with 1 tablespoon maple syrup and 1½ teaspoons dark soy sauce, and sprinkle it with 1½ tablespoons toasted coconut flakes. Repeat the process with the rest of the batter and ingredients to make 3 more eggs-in-a-hole.

OATMEAL BREAD POPARA

serves 3 to 4 for breakfast

1½ cups unsweetened almond
    milk
¼ teaspoon freshly grated
    nutmeg, or ⅜ teaspoon ground
¼ teaspoon vanilla extract

3 tablespoons unsalted butter
⅔ stale loaf of Nutmeg-Spiced
    Oatmeal Bread (see page 42), cut
    into 1-inch cubes (4 to 4½ cups)
3 teaspoons dark brown sugar

¼ teaspoon salt
1 tablespoon almond butter
¼ cup whole almonds, toasted
    (see page 26) and coarsely
    chopped

This is loosely based on a recipe for a Serbian *popara*, a savory breakfast porridge made with stale bread, water or milk, butter, and a soft white cow's-milk cheese. With at least half a loaf of my Nutmeg-Spiced Oatmeal Bread on my counter the day after I'd baked it, I wanted to see how it might translate into that porridge. The *popara* recipes I found looked a tad austere (I couldn't help but think of Oliver Twist and his gruel), although they do use butter, which I consider proof of pleasure taking and good taste. Rather than boiling the bread, I toasted it in my skillet, before letting it soak up enhanced almond milk. I don't know how this would be received in Central Asia, but I think young Oliver would ask for more, twice over, at least.

1   In a measuring cup, stir the almond milk, nutmeg, and vanilla and set aside.

2   Preheat a 10-inch cast-iron skillet on the stovetop, gradually raising the heat from low to medium. When the skillet is hot, add the butter. When it is melted and sizzling, add the cubes of stale bread, stirring them until well coated. Sprinkle 2 teaspoons of the brown sugar over the bread cubes, followed by the salt, and continue to stir. The sugar will melt and combine with the butter.

3   Let the bread cubes cook for 5 minutes, until they are nicely toasted and their edges are well caramelized. Reduce the heat to medium-low and pour the spiced almond milk into the pan. It will sizzle and bubble up, then settle into a simmer. Reduce the heat further, if necessary. Simmer the bread in the liquid for 7 minutes, or until the bread cubes absorb the almond milk, begin to break down, and, in turn, thicken whatever liquid hasn't cooked down or been absorbed. You will be left with a chunky porridge and no liquid in the pan.

4   Remove the skillet from the heat and stir the almond butter into the porridge. Taste it for sweetness, and, if you want, sprinkle the remaining 1 teaspoon brown sugar over the top and stir again to combine. Garnish with the toasted almonds and serve hot.

FARL FRITTATA WITH HALLOUMI

serves 4 for lunch or 6 to 8 for a snack

6 large eggs

½ teaspoon salt, plus more to taste

1 tablespoon fresh marjoram leaves, torn if large

1 tablespoon fresh thyme leaves

1 tablespoon chopped fresh dill

¼ loaf Irish Soda Farls (see page 38), or 2 cups bite-size pieces stale country loaf or ciabatta

1 tablespoon olive oil

¾ cup cubed halloumi (1 by 1 by ½ inch)

Best-quality extra-virgin olive oil, for drizzling

Coarsely ground black pepper, for garnish

A frittata is Italy's tart-shaped answer to the omelet. It's a group-friendly dish that can be readily shared and presents quite elegantly. It's also an excellent way to use up extra produce, or, as chef Jody Williams of Buvette taught me, leftover loaves. Scattered amid the light, springy, cooked eggs, hunks of crusty bread absorb some of the yolky batter and become custardy. Halloumi's creaminess runs through the sunny yellow surface, while a liberal use of fresh herbs offsets all of the richness of the dish.

1 Preheat the oven to 400°F. Preheat a 10-inch cast-iron skillet on the stovetop, gradually raising the heat from low to medium-low.

2 In a medium bowl, using a fork, whisk together the eggs, salt, marjoram, thyme, and dill. Tear the farls into large bite-size chunks and drop them into the egg mixture.

3 When the skillet is hot, add the olive oil. It should sizzle. Pour the frittata mixture into the pan. Gently jiggle the pan to evenly distribute the bread and herbs. Increase the heat to high and cook for 1 to 3 minutes, until the bottom of the frittata sets and is evenly pale gold (but not brown). While it's setting, use a spatula to loosen the batter from the sides of the skillet. This will prevent sticking and slightly lift the frittata, allowing it to cool off so it stays loose. At this point, the top should still be liquid.

4 Evenly dot the frittata with the halloumi cubes and move the pan to the oven for 5 to 8 minutes so the cheese can soften and the top of the frittata can set. Keep an eye on it; you don't want it any darker than a deep gold. (Browning on the edges is okay, but should otherwise be avoided.)

5 Garnish the finished frittata with a generous drizzle of extra-virgin olive oil, making sure to get the craggy chunks of bread, and add as much freshly ground pepper and, if necessary, extra salt as you like. Serve hot or at room temperature.

MIGAS WITH SWEET POTATO RUSKS & CHINESE SAUSAGE

serves 3

4 cups (6- to 7-day-old) Sweet Potato Rusks (see page 126), torn into ½-inch pieces

2½ links dried Chinese sausage (*lap cheong*), sliced on an angle into ¼-inch-wide pieces (¾ cup)

1 bunch (about 7) scallions, dark green parts only, left whole and trimmed to fit the pan

1 tablespoon unsalted butter

3 large eggs

½ cup canola oil

1 garlic clove, lightly crushed

1 teaspoon salt

2 tablespoons coarsely chopped fresh cilantro

1½ teaspoons garam masala

1 cup halved seedless red grapes

Zest of 1 small lime

1 tablespoon rice wine vinegar

Hoisin sauce

Sambal oelek or your preferred chili paste

My so-called *migas* is not so very Spanish, although its Aragonese forebear, which I hoarded at chefs Alex Raij and Eder Montero's Brooklyn restaurant La Vara, is. I use *lap cheong*, a type of Chinese sausage in place of chorizo, because I am absolutely mad about the funky, dried sticks of porky dynamite. Their sweet pungency and aromatic complexity are in keeping with the flavors of my Sweet Potato Rusks, which provide the base for this scramble. Fried eggs turn it into a more complete meal, and once cut into, their soft, runny yolks act as a voluptuous sauce. This is one of the dishes in this book that I find myself longing for often. If you don't have a batch of sweet potato rusks lying around, you can substitute store-bought challah or brioche, or even Parker House rolls.

1   Preheat the oven to 200°F. Spread the bread pieces out on a baking sheet and bake for about 1 hour, until the chunks have dried out and crisped up. Remove the sheet from the oven and set it aside to cool.

2   Meanwhile, preheat a 10-inch cast-iron skillet on the stovetop, gradually raising the heat from low to medium. Once the pan is hot, add the sausage and sauté for 3 to 4 minutes, until crispy. Transfer the sausage to a small bowl and set aside, then drain the rendered fat into another small bowl and reserve.

3   Raise the oven temperature to 450°F. Wipe the skillet out, blotting any excess sausage fat. Place the scallions in the pan, drizzle them with 1 teaspoon of the reserved fat, and cook in the oven for 10 to 15 minutes, until they've begun to brown and their edges turn crispy. Remove the skillet from the oven and transfer the scallions to a small plate. Once

(RECIPE CONTINUES)

they're cool enough to handle, slice them into 1-inch batons and set aside.

4   Wipe the skillet out and return it to the stovetop over medium heat.

5   In a large nonstick or well-seasoned carbon-steel skillet (see On Frying Eggs, right), melt the butter over medium heat. Once it is melted and sizzling, crack the eggs, separately, into the pan and fry them for 2 to 3 minutes, until their whites are cooked through and their yolks just set; you want the latter to remain soft. Transfer the fried eggs to a plate and set them aside.

6   Return the cast-iron skillet to the stove and preheat it, gradually raising the heat from low to medium. Once the pan is hot, add the canola oil. When the oil is hot, add the crushed garlic and cook it for a minute or two, flipping it over until it's golden brown on both sides (be careful not to let it burn). Remove and discard it.

7   Reduce the heat to low. Add the toasted bread pieces and salt to the pan, stirring to evenly coat the bread with oil. Add the cilantro and cook, tossing or stirring with a wooden spatula or spoon, for 5 to 7 minutes, until the croutons are golden and crispy. Add the garam masala, stir to incorporate, then remove the pan from the heat.

8   Quickly add the sausage, grapes, scallions, and lime zest and toss or stir to distribute everything evenly. Add the vinegar and toss or stir to combine. Place the fried eggs over the mixture and drizzle with about 2 tablespoons hoisin sauce and about 1 teaspoon sambal oelek (more or less of each, according to your taste).

9   Serve immediately, distributing the migas among 3 plates, making sure there's an egg on each.

On Frying Eggs

We can all agree that the cast-iron skillet is a versatile surface capable of so many culinary feats, but it's not the best for egg cookery. It's hard on the poor dears, and although it's relatively nonstick—and it becomes increasingly so with regular use and seasoning—it's not as nonstick as other materials.

My favorite pan for frying eggs is not the expected Teflon, which definitely gets the job done. It's a well-seasoned carbon-steel pan—specifically the one hand-crafted in Seattle by the husband-and-wife duo of Blu Skillet. The carbon steel heats evenly, which cast iron does not, and this is better for cooking more delicate items, like eggs. If cast iron is all you have, you can still use it to fry eggs. Just make sure the pan is well seasoned, remember to preheat it first, and watch it so you don't get an overcooked, solid yolk.

PAN-ROASTED BISCUIT GNOCCHI

serves 3

1½ cups dried-out, day-old biscuit crumbs (from about 7 biscuits or 1 recipe Sorghum Biscuits, page 98; see Notes)

6 tablespoons grated Parmesan cheese

8 gratings fresh nutmeg

½ teaspoon fine salt

¼ teaspoon ground white pepper

¾ cup vegetable stock, at room temperature

3 large egg yolks

¾ cup "00" flour (see Notes)

1 tablespoon kosher salt

1 tablespoon unsalted butter

1 tablespoon olive oil

Pan-Fried Sage Pesto (see page 207), for serving

½ teaspoon lemon zest, for garnishing

At Hog & Hominy in Memphis, Tennessee, I had a perfectly executed *gnocchi al pomodoro*, true to form, except for one difference: the dough had been made using stale biscuits, an ingenious way to transform scraps into a soul-satisfying plateful. Andrew Ticer and Michael Hudman's Southern-Grandma-Meets-Italian-Nonna pasta inspired me. Full of confidence, I was excited to take my Sorghum Biscuits in a similar direction with butter, sage, pine nuts, and grated Parmesan. For the life of me, I couldn't figure out how they made those soft, fluffy dumplings. I caved and asked for help. Using their procedure, I increased the flavor factor with grated fresh nutmeg, ground white pepper, and a deep-green pesto. If you don't feel like making that sauce yourself, you could get a store-bought basil number. The gnocchi won't suffer for it . . . too much.

1   In a large bowl, using a wooden spoon, stir the biscuit crumbs, Parmesan, nutmeg, fine salt, and white pepper together to combine. Place the vegetable stock in a small bowl, add the egg yolks, and whisk until incorporated. Make a well in the seasoned biscuit crumbs, pour the yolk-stock mixture into the center, and stir with a wooden spoon or use your hands to combine the wet and dry ingredients.

2   Add ½ cup of the flour and use your hands to gently incorporate it to form a dough. If it's too wet, continue to add the flour, 1 tablespoon at a time, until it comes together and is smooth. Give it a quick knead, making sure not to overwork it or you'll get heavy gnocchi, and let it rest, covered with a kitchen towel, for 1 hour at room temperature.

3   Turn the dough out onto a clean work surface. You shouldn't have to flour it, but if you're at all worried, put a Silpat mat down first. Divide the dough into quarters and, working with one at a time, use your fingers

(RECIPE CONTINUES)

to roll each quarter out into a snakelike rod 1 inch wide and 6 to 8 inches long. As you roll the rod and it lengthens, move your fingers out toward the edges and continue to roll until you've reached the desired diameter. Cut the rod into ½-inch portions using a bench scraper or a sharp knife. Using a fork or your thumb, press lightly into each gnocchi to flatten its top. Place the shaped gnocchi onto a parchment paper–lined baking sheet and cover them with plastic wrap or a kitchen towel until you're ready to cook them. If you're not cooking them immediately—the same day, ideally, or else the following day—you can freeze them in an airtight container for up to 1 month.

4   When you're ready to cook the gnocchi, fill a medium pot (about 4-quart capacity) with water and add the kosher salt. Bring the water to a boil over high heat. When the water seems close to boiling, fill a large bowl with ice and water. Place a colander in the bowl; you should have enough water in the bowl to fill the colander.

5   Once the water is boiling, add the gnocchi, sliding them off the baking sheet. After about 3 minutes, the gnocchi should float up to the surface. Using a slotted spoon, drain the gnocchi as you lift them from the water and transfer them to the colander to stop the cooking. Using your slotted spoon, transfer the gnocchi from the colander to the (relined) baking sheet. If you aren't planning to serve them right away, you can set them

aside, covered with a kitchen towel, for a few hours or else freeze them for later use. (They don't need to be thawed before finishing.)

6   When you're ready to serve the gnocchi, preheat a 10-inch cast-iron skillet on the stovetop, gradually increasing the heat from low to medium. When the pan is hot, add the butter and olive oil. When the butter is melted and sizzling, tilt to coat and add half the gnocchi. Toast the gnocchi, using a spatula to flip them over so each side can get golden, about 2 minutes per side. Transfer the finished gnocchi to a plate to keep warm while you toast the remaining boiled gnocchi in the skillet. You shouldn't need to add more butter or oil.

7   To serve, divide the gnocchi into 3 portions and top each with about 1½ tablespoons of pesto. Garnish with a grating of lemon zest.

NOTES

• To dry the biscuits out, put them on a baking sheet in the oven overnight at 150°F (or, if your oven doesn't go that low, as close to that as possible, but no higher than 200°F). Place the dried-out biscuits in the food processor and pulse until you're left with fine crumbs.

• Ticer and Hudman use Italian "00" (*doppio zero*) flour for their recipe. It's more finely ground than the all-purpose stuff and yields softer gnocchi. But you can use all-purpose flour if that's what you've got.

GINGERBREAD CHALLAH BOSTOCK

makes 6 or 7

3 slices stale Challah D'Epices
(see page 149), 2 inches thick

Almond Syrup (recipe follows)
Frangipane (recipe follows)

1 teaspoon butter

There is nothing at all wrong with French toast. But, ironically enough, the French themselves have something even better—*bostock*. It's self-contained, for one—the stale bread soaks in an almond-flavored syrup, so you don't need to sauce it and can carry it with you. And you get a free gift with purchase: a frangipane cap. The fluffy butter-and-almond cream is slathered on the syrupy bread and, once baked, forms a delicate crispy crust. This particular bostock is special on two counts: 1) It features that headily spiced gingerbread challah, and 2) Lily Freedman ratcheted up the aromatics with a black-pepper curveball.

When writing a cookbook, it is customary and advised—if not mandatory—to make sure someone else tests your recipes after you've done so yourself. Lily was that someone else. She performed her job painstakingly, applying her exceptional palate, uncanny—possibly photographic—memory, and frighteningly sharp attention to detail to each new flatbread or sweet I sent her way. I thought it would be nice—just this once—if we swapped roles. She would turn my challah into *bostock*, then I would test her recipe. With her frangipane, she knocked it out of the park. Its ginger and clove echo that of the bread, and then there's that lingering tease of a peppery tickle.

1   Preheat the oven to 350°F with a 10-inch cast-iron skillet in it.

2   Using a 2¼-inch biscuit cutter, cut the challah slices into 6 or 7 rounds, depending on how much usable surface area you have. Dunk each round into the Almond Syrup until it is fully soaked, then give it a gentle squeeze to expel the excess liquid and place it on a large plate with the others. Spread about 2 tablespoons of the Frangipane over the top of each round to create a thick layer. Try not to let the frangipane go over the edges of the challah to avoid excessive spillage onto the skillet during baking and make cleanup easier.

3   Remove the skillet from the oven and add the butter, tilting to coat. Place the rounds in the pan and return it to the oven to bake for about 20 minutes, until the frangipane begins to harden and turn golden. Using a spatula, immediately transfer the rounds from the skillet to a wire rack to cool.

(RECIPE CONTINUES)

ALMOND SYRUP
makes about 1 cup

¼ cup leftover challah glaze (see page 149;
   see Notes)
¼ cup packed light brown sugar
2 tablespoons buckwheat honey
1 teaspoon almond extract
½ teaspoon vanilla extract
½ teaspoon salt
5 gratings of fresh nutmeg

In a small saucepan, combine all the ingredients
plus 1 cup water and bring to a boil, stirring
occasionally with a whisk, over medium heat.
Remove the syrup from the heat, whisk again
to make sure it's well combined, and let it cool
completely before use. (This can be made up to a
week in advance and kept in a sealed container
in the refrigerator.)

> **NOTES**
> - The challah needs to be seriously
>   stale—at *least* 3 days old—for the syrup
>   to absorb rather than turn your bread to
>   mush.
>
> - If, for whatever reason, you don't have
>   leftover glaze, you can make another
>   batch, up to a week in advance, and
>   refrigerate it. If your glaze has separated
>   in the refrigerator, bring it back to room
>   temperature and stir to re-combine.

FRANGIPANE
makes about 1 cup

3 tablespoons unsalted butter, at room temperature
1 tablespoon sugar
Scant ½ cup packed almond paste, broken into
   1-inch or teaspoon-size chunks
1 large egg
1½ tablespoons unbleached all-purpose flour
½ teaspoon ground cloves
½ teaspoon ground ginger
¼ teaspoon freshly ground black pepper
¼ teaspoon salt

1 In the bowl of a stand mixer fitted with the
paddle, beat the butter on low speed for
1 minute or so until it's smooth and fluffy.
Add the sugar and mix for about 30 seconds
to incorporate. Increase the speed to medium
and mix for 2 to 3 minutes, until fluffy. Add
the almond paste and beat for another 2 to
3 minutes, until the almond paste combines
with the creamed butter and sugar and the
mixture resembles torn pieces of Play-Doh.

2 Add the egg and continue to beat for another
30 seconds, until incorporated into a smooth
paste. Return the machine to low speed and
add the flour, spices, pepper, and salt and
mix for a few seconds. Increase the speed
to medium and mix for about 30 seconds,
until the mixture looks like a light, creamy
frosting. If necessary, using a rubber spatula,
scrape down the sides of the bowl and mix
again to make sure any additional flour is
thoroughly combined.

RASPEACH COBBLER

serves 6 to 8

1½ pints raspberries (see Note)

3 cups sliced peaches (about ¼ inch wide)

½ cup granulated sugar

½ cup light brown sugar

2½ tablespoons tapioca flour

⅛ teaspoon salt

1 tablespoon fresh lemon juice

1 teaspoon vanilla extract

1 recipe Sorghum Biscuit dough (see page 98)

1 tablespoon unsalted butter

2 tablespoons turbinado sugar

1½ teaspoons aniseeds (see Note)

Vanilla ice cream and toasted hazelnuts (or else hazelnut gelato), for serving

As for the obvious—sweet—cobbler preparation, the coupling of peaches and raspberries isn't anything new, but it's unarguably sublime. Sprinkled with crunchy turbinado sugar and licoricelike aniseeds, Sorghum Biscuit dough provides the covering, and I dropped small blobs of it into the fruit sizzling in the hot pan, so that it resembles, as my friend Gabriella pointed out, cobblestones.

1   Preheat the oven to 375°F with a 10-inch cast-iron skillet in it.

2   In a large bowl, combine the raspberries and peaches. In a small bowl, whisk together the sugars, tapioca flour, and salt. Pour the mixture over the fruit, followed by the lemon juice and vanilla. Using a wooden spoon or rubber spatula, gently mix everything together to evenly coat the fruit without breaking it. Set the bowl aside while you make the biscuit topping.

3   Make the biscuit dough without refrigerating it (you will be topping the cobbler with it right away).

4   Remove the hot skillet from the oven. Place the butter in the pan and let it melt, brushing it to coat the bottom and sides. Using the wooden spoon or spatula, ease the fruit mixture into the skillet along with any syrup that may have accumulated in the bowl.

5   Using your fingers, tear off small gobs of the biscuit dough and dot the surface of the fruit with them. Sprinkle the turbinado sugar and aniseeds over the top and bake the cobbler for 40 minutes, until the top is golden brown and the fruit is bubbling. Remove the cobbler from the oven and serve warm, with vanilla ice cream and toasted hazelnuts.

NOTE This cobbler doesn't have to include raspberries—blueberries, cherries, plums, or figs would all make excellent companions for the peaches. Dried fruit reconstituted in hot water or brandy is another option. And if you don't like aniseed, or want to try something new, poppy or sesame seeds are up to the task. So are crushed peppercorns—black, pink, or Sichuan.

FOCACCIA PANCOTTO

serves 3

¼ loaf stale (up to 3-day-old) focaccia, sliced ½ inch thick, cut into 1-inch cubes
2 tablespoons extra-virgin olive oil, plus more for drizzling
1 clove garlic, lightly crushed

1 small parsnip (5 to 6 ounces), cut into ¼-inch dice (about 1 cup)
1 large leek, trimmed and sliced into ribbons and rinsed thoroughly in a colander
½ teaspoon salt, plus more to taste

⅛ teaspoon dried chili flakes
½ cup grated Sicilian Caciocavallo (or pecorino) cheese
2 cups arugula
Flat-leaf parsley, for garnish

When I'm feeling run-down or blue, I crave *pappa al pomodoro*, a hearty Tuscan tomato soup thickened with bread. One afternoon, in search of solace and in possession of some uneaten focaccia, I became determined to turn the doughy leftovers into *pappa*, using not a pot but my trusty skillet. There was one major glitch: the *pomodoro*. Whether or not tomatoes are bad for cast iron is up in the air, but there's no doubt that cast iron is bad for tomatoes. Any kind of reducing or other low and slow cooking will leave them with a metallic and bitter aftertaste. I held out hope for a commendable alternative, and I found it in *pancotto*. Eaten throughout The Boot, its name literally translates to "cooked bread," and its preparation varies in Italy from region to region and household to household. Stale bread appears to be the only nonnegotiable.

I chose leek and parsnip to flavor the cooking liquid and added some chili flakes for heat. The focaccia drank up the vegetal broth and began to fall apart. I pulled the resulting porridge from the heat and stirred in Sicilian

Caciocavallo, a type of pecorino produced in southern Italy. Next, I heaped on my favorite leaf, arugula. Wilted by the heat of the soup, its pepperiness balanced the sweetness of the earthy parsnip and the oniony leek, and the saltiness of the focaccia and cheese. Finally, I piled on grassy, green parsley for brightness—aesthetic and gustatory. With this bowlful of comfort, I proved to myself, and now, I hope, to you, that it's possible to make soup in a cast-iron skillet, and to do it well.

1   Preheat the oven to 200°F with a 10-inch cast-iron skillet in it. When the pan is hot, add the bread in one layer and bake it until the chunks have dried out and crisped. You just want to dehydrate them; you don't want them to darken. Remove the skillet from the oven and transfer the bread to a bowl while you work on the rest.

2   Place the empty, oven-warm skillet on the stove over medium heat. Give the pan a

couple of minutes to get hotter and add the olive oil. Once the oil is hot, add the crushed garlic and cook it for a minute or two, flipping it over, until it's golden brown on both sides (be careful not to let it burn). Remove and discard it.

3   Reduce the heat to medium-low and add the parsnip and leek along with a pinch of salt. Using a spatula or wooden spoon, stir the vegetables to coat them evenly in the oil, then sweat them for about 10 minutes, stirring a couple of times throughout the process, until they begin to look dewy and start to soften around the edges. If it seems as though they're in danger of browning, reduce the heat.

4   Add the chili flakes and 2 cups of water to the skillet and raise the heat to medium to bring the mixture to a boil. Reduce the heat to medium-low, or low, to bring the liquid to a simmer for about 10 minutes, until the parsnip is cooked through.

5   Add the bread with 2 to 3 tablespoons more water and cook for 2 to 3 minutes, until the bread has begun to absorb the liquid and turned soft. Using your spatula or wooden spoon, mush the bread to help break it down and incorporate it into the vegetable base. At this point, the mixture should begin to resemble porridge.

6   Add ½ cup water to the pan, continuing to simmer. As the mixture cooks and absorbs liquid, add more water, 1 to 2 tablespoons at a time, up to another ½ to ⅔ cup, until you have the desired consistency (see Notes).

Remove the pan from the stove, add ¼ cup of the cheese, and stir to incorporate as it melts into the soup. Add ¼ teaspoon salt and stir, again, to combine. Add the arugula and stir it into the soup to mix and wilt it. Add the remaining ¼ teaspoon salt, as needed, to taste.

7   Spoon the soup into 3 bowls. Drizzle extra-virgin olive oil over each. Sprinkle 1 tablespoon plus 1 teaspoon cheese (per bowl) on top and garnish with the parsley leaves.

NOTES

• Potatoes, white or sweet—or in combination—can stand in for parsnips; so can butternut squash or salsify, and I think charred, pan-roasted broccoli would be another way to go. Onions are easily swapped in for leeks.

• The cheese is interchangeable, too, so long as it's salty and good for grating. You could work with chicory, or turnip or mustard greens, instead of arugula. And you could garnish with sorrel or chervil at the very end.

• You are welcome to use vegetable or chicken stock here, but I recommend water, so that you don't muddle the flavor you've coaxed out of the vegetables.

• Once it starts to fall apart, the focaccia will behave like a thickening agent. You should add as much, or as little, water to the resulting porridge to achieve the consistency you desire. I like a thicker, almost stewlike soup. Some will want a thinner, brothier product.

NYC RAREBIT SANDWICH

serves 2

APPLE AND ONION SAUTÉ

1 tablespoon unsalted butter

1 cup julienned onion

1 cup julienned peeled apple

Kosher salt

Cayenne pepper

TOPPING

2 teaspoons best-quality Dijon
mustard

1½ teaspoons ketchup

1½ tablespoons stout

1 tablespoon unsalted butter

¾ teaspoon Worcestershire
sauce, plus more as needed

1 cup plus 1 tablespoon grated
cheddar cheese

1 egg yolk

2 English Muffins, My Way (see
page 134), split in half

This sandwich references the world's most perfect hangover food, the UK's Welsh rarebit. Toasted English muffins drenched in molten cheddar perfumed with beer and Worcestershire sauce hold a mixture of sautéed apples and onions. It's messy, as it should be. Take an obnoxiously large bite, let the cheesy lava dribble down your chin, and chase it with a hair-of-the-dog pint of Guinness—or maybe a Brooklyn-brewed stout to honor the Big Apple, where me and my rarebit were born.

1   **Prepare the sauté:** Preheat a 10-inch cast-iron skillet on the stovetop, gradually raising the heat from low to medium-high. When the pan is hot, add the butter. When it is melted and sizzling, add the onion and cook for about 7 minutes, so it softens and begins to color.

2   Add the apple and sauté for about 5 minutes more, until the onion is golden brown, the apple has softened, and their flavors have melded together. Transfer the mixture to a heatproof bowl and season with salt and cayenne. Set it aside while you make the rarebit topping.

3   **Make the topping:** In a small saucepan, combine the mustard, ketchup, stout, butter, and Worcestershire and heat over low heat until the butter has melted, whisking to combine. Add the cheese and, using the whisk, continue to stir, so it melts and incorporates. The mixture will be a bit lumpy, although the whisk will help smooth it out somewhat. Do not let it come to a boil.

4   Once the cheese has melted, taste and adjust the seasoning as needed, then take the pan off the heat. If it's hot, allow the mixture to cool until it's just slightly warm; you don't want it to solidify. Using a whisk, beat the egg yolk into the cheese mixture until it's smooth.

5   Preheat the 10-inch cast-iron skillet on the stovetop, gradually raising the heat from low to medium-high. When it is hot, place both halves of an English muffin facedown in the pan for about 2 minutes, to toast and begin to brown.

6   Once the inside of each half is toasted, flip it over and place 2 tablespoons of the rarebit topping on the toasted interiors. Let the muffin halves continue to cook for about 2 minutes more, until the cheese mixture is bubbling. Using a spatula, transfer them to a plate and place a heaping of the Apple and Onion Sauté on top of the bottom cheese-covered half. Gently flip the top cheese-covered half over to cover the sandwich. Repeat this process with the second split English muffin.

EGGPLANT PANZANELLA WITH FOCACCIA

serves 3

SALAD

1 small eggplant, cut into 1-inch
    cubes (about 2½ cups)

½ tablespoon kosher salt

⅜ loaf stale (up to 3-day-old)
    focaccia (see page 142), cut
    into 1-inch cubes (5 to 6 cups)

2 garlic cloves: 1 sliced in half,
    1 lightly crushed

¼ red onion, thinly sliced

1½ tablespoons olive oil

1 medium cucumber, cut into
    1-inch cubes (about 1½ cups)

1 ripe medium tomato, cut into
    large bite-size chunks

½ teaspoon fine salt, plus more
    to taste

Freshly ground black pepper

VINAIGRETTE

2 tablespoons rice wine vinegar

¼ teaspoon fine salt

1½ teaspoons maple syrup

¼ cup extra-virgin olive oil

Freshly ground black pepper

Fresh mint leaves, for garnish

Fresh basil leaves, for garnish

Bread is the raison d'être for any panzanella, old-style or newfangled. The first of these salads is a more authentic take. It starts with Michelle Rizzolo's olive oil–enriched focaccia and features the usual supporting actors—tomato, cucumber, basil, and red onion—along with a special guest star: crispy-skinned, melty-fleshed eggplant.

1   Make the salad: Preheat the oven to 200°F. In a colander set over a bowl, toss the eggplant with the kosher salt, making sure all the cubes are evenly coated. Let the eggplant sit and drain for at least 30 minutes and up to 1½ hours. Rinse the eggplant under cold water and pat it dry with a kitchen towel or paper towels, pressing out any excess water as you go.

2   While the eggplant is draining, spread the focaccia cubes on a baking sheet in a single layer and bake until the bread has dried out and crisped up. Remove the baking sheet from the oven and rub each warm cube with the raw garlic halves before transferring the bread to a large bowl so it can cool while you work on the rest. Add the garlic halves to the bowl, too, so they can continue to flavor the bread.

3   While the focaccia cubes are in the oven, place the red onion slices in a small strainer submerged in a bowl filled with ice water. Let them soak in the cold bath until you're ready to add them to the salad.

4 Preheat a 10-inch cast-iron skillet on the stove, gradually raising the heat from low to medium. When the pan is hot, add the olive oil and tilt to coat. Once the oil is hot, add the crushed garlic and cook it for a minute or two, flipping it over, until it's golden brown (be careful not to let it burn) on both sides. Remove and discard it. Add the eggplant cubes to the pan and sauté for 10 minutes, stirring from time to time, until the flesh has softened and turned golden brown.

5 Transfer the cooked eggplant to a large salad bowl and let it cool for 5 minutes. Add the focaccia cubes—leaving the raw garlic behind—followed by the cucumber and tomato. Drain the red onion, pat it dry, and add it to the salad bowl. Using your hands, a wooden spoon, or a rubber spatula, gently mix the ingredients together to evenly distribute them. Add the salt and 3 grinds of pepper and mix again to combine.

6 **Make the vinaigrette:** In a small bowl, whisk together the vinegar, fine salt, and maple syrup to combine. Whisk in the extra-virgin olive oil until emulsified. Add 3 grinds of pepper to the vinaigrette and whisk again to incorporate. Taste and adjust the seasonings, as needed.

7 **Assemble the salad:** Drizzle about half the vinaigrette over the salad and mix to incorporate. If you prefer a wetter, more heavily dressed salad, you can add more vinaigrette to suit your taste.

8 Let the panzanella sit for at least 30 minutes and up to 4 hours so the flavors can marinate and the bread can soak up the vinaigrette. Right before serving, tear the fresh mint and basil leaves (about 5 each) into the salad and mix to combine. Taste the panzanella and adjust the seasoning, adding more salt and pepper as needed.

PANISSE PANZANELLA WITH WILTED &
RAW LETTUCES, PAGE 192

EGGPLANT PANZANELLA WITH
FOCACCIA, PAGE 188

PANISSE PANZANELLA
WITH WILTED & RAW LETTUCES

serves 4 as a salad or side dish

VINAIGRETTE

¼ cup plus 2 tablespoons extra-
virgin olive oil

4 garlic cloves, aggressively
smashed

3 anchovy fillets

2 tablespoons mild red wine
vinegar, plus more to taste

Salt

Freshly ground black pepper

SALAD

2 tablespoons plus 2 teaspoons
olive oil

½ batch Green Pea Panisse (see
page 47), cut into 1-inch cubes
(about 4 cups; see Note)

Salt

2 tablespoons unsalted butter

3 tablespoons minced shallot

5 cups torn Boston lettuce

4 cups torn escarole

1 tablespoon chopped fresh dill

1 tablespoon chopped fresh mint
leaves

3 tablespoons fresh or thawed
frozen peas

3 tablespoons wasabi peas

Freshly ground black pepper

Made with a less obvious "crouton" candidate—
leftover Green Pea Panisse is a true celebration
of spring. There are a few steps, sure; but each
is quick and easy and can be done in your trusty
10-inch pan.

You will learn three new cast-iron tricks:
preparing a warm vinaigrette, charring
escarole, and wilting lettuce. Of course, you can
also do a cheat version where you leave all the
torn greens raw, keep the herbs, and use all the
dressing. Either way, don't forget the garnishes,
because they bring the pea flavor to the fore
and add some sharper textural contrasts to the
subtler ones already in the bowl.

1   Make the vinaigrette: Gradually raising the
temperature from low to medium-high, heat
2 tablespoons of the extra-virgin olive oil
in a 10-inch cast-iron skillet. When the oil
is hot, add the smashed garlic cloves to the
skillet and cook for 1 minute so the garlic
toasts and begins to lightly brown without
burning. Remove the pan from the heat and
add the anchovies. They will immediately
begin to melt. Using a wooden spoon, stir the
anchovies and the garlic to break them apart
and evenly distribute them in the oil. If the
garlic isn't breaking up, use a fork to mash it
into the oil so it incorporates.

2   Add the remaining ¼ cup extra-virgin olive
oil and the vinegar to the skillet. (Add an
extra teaspoon of vinegar if you prefer a

more acidic vinaigrette.) Season the dressing with salt and pepper and return it to the stovetop. Bring it to a simmer over medium-low heat. Pour the finished vinaigrette into a bowl kept near the hot stove or else into a small saucepan placed over low heat on the stove so it's warm upon serving.

3   **Make the salad:** Wipe out the skillet, place it back on the stovetop over low heat, and add 2 tablespoons of the oil. Gradually raise the heat to medium-high to get the oil hot. Add the panisse cubes and toast them for 5 to 7 minutes, until their exteriors begin to crisp up again and become more golden. Place the finished croutons on a warm, paper towel–lined plate and sprinkle them with a pinch of salt. Set them aside, near the hot stovetop, to stay warm while you prepare the lettuces.

4   Wipe out the skillet, place it back on the stove over low heat, and add the butter. As the butter melts, gradually increase the heat to medium-high and, when the butter is sizzling, add the shallot to the pan and sauté for 30 seconds so it can begin to soften. Add 4 cups of the lettuce. Sauté the leaves quickly, stirring or tossing them continuously for 1 minute, so they are all lightly coated with the butter and just wilted (not soggy). Remove the lettuce and shallot from the pan, draining as much of the cooking liquid as possible, and place them in a small bowl. Season the lettuce with salt and set the bowl aside.

5   Wipe out the skillet, place it back on the stove over low heat, and add 1 teaspoon of the oil, tilting to coat. Meanwhile, place 3 cups of the torn escarole in a medium bowl, making sure the leaves are completely dry. Toss them with the remaining 1 teaspoon oil. Gradually increase the heat under the skillet to medium-high, and when the pan and oil are hot, add the escarole, using a spoon or spatula to spread the leaves out to fill the skillet. Leave the escarole to cook for about 5 minutes, so it toasts on one side. Give the pan a quick toss to move the finished leaves around before placing them in a small bowl.

6   **Assemble the salad:** Place the wilted Boston lettuce and shallot in a large salad bowl, followed by the remaining 1 cup raw escarole. Next, add the pan-roasted escarole, followed by the remaining 1 cup raw lettuce. Drizzle half the vinaigrette (about ¼ cup) over the contents of the bowl, making sure to include some of the anchovy and garlic sediment, and toss everything together. Add the panisse croutons, dill, and mint and toss everything again. Garnish with the raw green peas and wasabi peas, season with salt and pepper to taste, and add more dressing, if necessary (it shouldn't be).

> **NOTE**   You could, alternatively, make the croutons fresh from the *panisse* batter, before preparing the dressing. If you opt for this method, place the just-cooked croutons in an oven-friendly pan covered with aluminum foil, and keep them warm in a warming drawer or a low-heated oven.

MY ALL-TIME FAVORITE STUFFING

serves 4 to 6 as a side

½ cup packed dried figs
    (5 to 6 figs)
1 cup apple cider (or more to
    cover the figs)
1 cup store-bought cooked whole
    peeled chestnuts

4 cups large hand-torn chunks
    of 1- to 2-day-old cornbread
    (see Note)
½ cup canned creamed corn
½ cup frozen or fresh corn
    kernels
1 tablespoon fresh thyme leaves
3 fresh sage leaves, coarsely torn

Salt
Freshly ground black pepper
1½ cups chicken or vegetable
    stock
6 tablespoons (¾ stick) unsalted
    butter, divided into 4 plus
    2 tablespoons, cubed, and kept
    separate

My family isn't big into Thanksgiving. This isn't much of a surprise—our head cook, my mother, thinks turkey's a waste of time, and I tend to agree. The last time we got together to celebrate the traditional way at my parents' house was over a decade ago. Mom deigned to roast the boring bird, and I bossily insisted on handling the stuffing because it's my favorite Thanksgiving food. I'd imagined the most perfect

version made of cornbread baked in a cast-iron skillet. Two cheater moves—the purchasing of canned creamed corn and preroasted and shelled chestnuts (desperate measures)—turned out to be the smartest things I could have done for my side dish, which lived up to my fantasy. A recipe seems almost perfunctory here. You're mostly putting some delicious things in a skillet, adding some stock and butter, and baking it all together.

1   Preheat the oven to 350°F.

2   Place the figs in a small saucepan with enough apple cider to cover them and bring to a simmer. Cook the figs for 5 minutes, then remove from the heat and let cool. Drain the liquid from the saucepan and coarsely dice the reconstituted figs. Set them aside.

3   Preheat a 10-inch cast-iron skillet on the stovetop, gradually raising the heat from low to medium-high. When the skillet is hot, add the chestnuts and toast them for 5 minutes, shaking the pan or stirring them often, making sure not to burn them.

4   Take the pan off the heat, place the toasted chestnuts on your cutting board, and wipe out the skillet. Coarsely chop the chestnuts and set them aside.

5   Put the skillet back on the stove and place it over low heat to stay warm. Meanwhile, in a large bowl, using your hands or a wooden spoon, combine the torn cornbread, chopped figs and chestnuts, creamed corn, corn kernels, thyme, and sage. Be gentle when mixing everything together. You want the ingredients to be well distributed, but you don't want the cornbread to fall apart. Season the mixture with salt and pepper.

6   Place the cornbread mixture in the skillet and pour the stock over and around it. Dot the top of the stuffing with 4 tablespoons of the cubed butter. Put the pan in the oven and bake for 45 minutes. After 30 minutes, dot the stuffing with the remaining 2 tablespoons cubed butter. Serve warm. Stored in a sealed container, leftovers can be refrigerated for up to 2 days and reheated.

NOTE Mom's Cornbread Revisited (page 66) was practically made for this dish. I had stuffing in mind when I developed the recipe! Its onions are a powerful ally of figs, chestnuts, thyme, and sage. You could use another cornbread, homemade or store-bought, but then you might want to consider adding some caramelized onions to the stuffing.

EGG SALAD MELT WITH ROASTED ASPARAGUS

serves 4 (makes 8 open-face sandwiches)

1 teaspoon unsalted butter

12 asparagus spears, trimmed to 7 to 8 inches, ends peeled as necessary

1½ teaspoons olive oil

⅛ teaspoon kosher salt

6 large eggs

4 teaspoons mayonnaise (preferably Duke's)

2 teaspoons Dijon mustard

¼ teaspoon freshly ground black pepper, plus more to taste

⅜ teaspoon fine salt, plus more to taste

½ tablespoon coarsely chopped fresh tarragon

8 untoasted Crumpets (see page 50)

½ cup packed grated Parmesan cheese

½ cup packed shredded low-moisture mozzarella

8 thin slices prosciutto

Unlike its sloppy sibling, the NYC Rarebit Sandwich (page 186), this tidy sandwich is open-face. I'd never seen egg salad pressed into service of a melt and wondered if it could be done. These musings coincided with the arrival of the season's first asparagus. I folded the crispy, cast-iron-roasted, chopped spears into the yolky, mayo-bound salad seasoned with Dijon mustard and fresh tarragon. I placed a small pile on each crumpet and smothered it with a combination of Parmesan and mozzarella. Then I ran it under the broiler to brown the cheese. You could stop there; it's already delicious—plus vegetarian. You could also keep going and fold a cold, thin slice of salty prosciutto over the melt right before you serve it.

1 Preheat the oven to 450°F with a 10-inch cast-iron skillet in it. When the pan is hot, remove it from the oven and place the butter in it to melt, tilting to coat. Place the asparagus in the pan, drizzle the spears with the olive oil, and sprinkle them with the kosher salt. Roast for 10 to 15 minutes, until they begin to brown and their tops crisp up a bit and darken. Using tongs, turn the asparagus over midway through roasting to get both sides evenly cooked.

2 Transfer the roasted asparagus to a cutting board and let them cool down so you can cut them. Slice them into ½-inch pieces. You should have about 1 cup. Set the chopped asparagus aside. Wipe out the skillet.

3 Place the eggs in a large pot and add water to cover by ¾ inch. Cook the eggs over high heat, stirring occasionally, for 15 to 20 minutes, until just before the water starts to boil. Remove the pot from the heat and let the eggs sit in the water, covered with a lid, for 9 minutes. Drain the water and run the eggs under cold water to prevent them from

cooking further. Peel the eggs and separate the whites and yolks, placing the latter in a medium bowl and the former in a small bowl. Use your hands to break the whites into uneven pieces.

4   In the medium bowl, using a fork, gently smash the yolks with the mayonnaise, mustard, pepper, and fine salt to form a paste. Fold the egg whites, then the asparagus, into the yolk mixture, evenly combining the ingredients and fluffing the salad as you go. Gently fold in the tarragon. Taste for seasoning and adjust as needed. You don't want to overwork it.

5   Preheat a 10-inch cast-iron skillet on the stovetop, gradually raising the heat from low to medium. With a rack placed 3 to 4 inches from the oven's ceiling, turn on the broiler. Once the pan is hot, place up to 3 Crumpets in it. Quickly top each with ¼ cup of the egg salad, followed by 1 tablespoon Parmesan and 1 tablespoon mozzarella.

6   Broil for 3 minutes, until the cheeses are browned and bubbling. Remove the pan from the oven and, using a spatula, place the crumpets on a serving platter or plate them individually, 2 per person. Repeat with the remaining Crumpets and egg salad. Place a thin slice of cold prosciutto over each and serve.

ROASTED VEGETABLE COBBLER

serves 4 to 5 as a light meal or 6 to 7 as a side dish

7 small to medium carrots,
scrubbed

1 medium to large fennel bulb

5 baby red, yellow, or orange bell
peppers, or 2 large red, yellow,
or orange peppers

2 teaspoons plus 1 tablespoon
olive oil

½ teaspoon kosher salt

1½ teaspoons fennel seeds

1 cup ¼-inch-diced Spanish or
yellow onion (about 1 medium
onion)

1 dried bay leaf

½ teaspoon freshly ground black
pepper

1 cup vegetable stock

½ cup heavy cream

¼ teaspoon fennel pollen

1 teaspoon honey

2 tablespoons coarsely chopped
fresh parsley, plus more for
garnish

½ teaspoon fine salt

½ recipe Spiced Butternut
Squash Biscuit dough (see
page 84) or savory biscuit
dough of your choice

Fennel fronds, for garnish
(optional)

Carrot greens, for garnish
(optional)

Butternut "Crème" (recipe
follows), for serving

Spiced Seeds (recipe follows), for
serving

While a fruit cobbler seems like a shoo-in for this kind of cookbook, its vegetable equivalent is probably not a foregone conclusion for most people. It was, for me, because I had half a batch's worth of unbaked Spiced Butternut Squash Biscuits in my fridge. I had leftover puréed roasted butternut squash in there, too, from that same recipe. Plus I'd toasted the gourd's seeds in the hopes of employing them as a future garnish. Putting all these remainders into one dish was the best way to use them up.

1   Prep the vegetables: Slice the carrots, on an angle, into 1½-inch rods, splitting thicker pieces in half lengthwise. Cut the fennel into roughly 1½ by 1½-inch pieces. If you are using large peppers, core and seed them before cutting them, lengthwise, into strips 2 inches wide.

2   Preheat the oven to 400°F. In a medium bowl, combine the carrots, fennel wedges, and bell peppers and, using your hands, toss with 2 teaspoons of the olive oil and the kosher salt to coat. Place the seasoned vegetables on a baking sheet and roast for 25 minutes, stirring the vegetables midway through cooking.

3 While the vegetables are roasting, start the sauce. Preheat a 10-inch cast-iron skillet on the stovetop, gradually raising the heat from low to medium-high. Once the pan is hot, add the fennel seeds and toast them for about 3 minutes, until they begin to pop and release a concentrated aroma.

4 Add the remaining 1 tablespoon olive oil and give it a few seconds to get hot. Add the onion, followed by the bay leaf and black pepper. Cook for 5 minutes, stirring occasionally with a wooden spatula, until the onion has softened and become translucent. Add the vegetable stock to the skillet; it should come to a boil almost immediately. Reduce the heat to medium-low and simmer for about 15 minutes, until the liquid in the pan has reduced by about half. Raise the heat to medium and add the heavy cream. Bring the liquid to a boil and lower the heat to medium-low. Simmer for about 25 minutes, until the liquid in the pan has reduced by half. If you push a wooden spatula through the mixture, the cream should have thickened enough so that it doesn't immediately run back into the cleared space left behind.

5 While the sauce is reducing, return to the roasted vegetables. Once they're ready, take the baking sheet out of the oven. Leave the oven on. Let the vegetables cool on the baking sheet for about 5 minutes, or until you can handle them. Transfer the baby peppers, if using, to a cutting board, remove their stems, and cut them into bite-size chunks, scraping away any seeds as necessary. Trim

any fennel core. Place the roasted vegetables in a medium bowl and toss with the fennel pollen, honey, and parsley.

6 When the sauce has reduced to the desired consistency, stir in ¼ teaspoon of the fine salt. Turn off the heat, remove the bay leaf, and add the roasted vegetables to the skillet. Using a wooden spatula, stir to combine. Add the remaining ¼ teaspoon fine salt and stir again to incorporate. Top the mixture with seven 2-inch rounds of raw biscuit dough, or, alternatively, you can apply the dough drop-style and place a few heaping tablespoons, in gobs, over the vegetables.

7 Put the skillet in the oven. Because the dough has a tendency to rise significantly and is sitting on top of all the vegetables, you should place the pan on a rack closer to the middle of the oven. Bake for 20 to 25 minutes, until the biscuits are cooked through.

8 Serve the cobbler in the skillet, garnishing it, if desired, with additional chopped parsley, fennel fronds, and carrot greens and placing the Butternut Crème and Spiced Seeds in separate serving dishes on the side, so people can dig in and top to their taste. Or plate it individually, in bowls, garnishing each with a dollop of Crème, a sprinkling of seeds, and, if you'd like, some of the fresh herb and/or vegetable greens. In addition to working as a light supper or lunch, it can function as a side dish, and would make an especially festive one for Thanksgiving.

(RECIPE CONTINUES)

BUTTERNUT "CRÈME"
makes about 1 cup

½ cup crème fraîche

½ cup puréed roasted butternut squash
  (see page 84)

2 tablespoons best-quality Dijon mustard

1 teaspoon honey

½ teaspoon salt

Place all the ingredients in a bowl and, using
a rubber spatula, fold them together until
completely incorporated.

SPICED SEEDS
makes about 1 cup

1 cup seeds from a butternut squash and pumpkin
  (see Note)

1 tablespoon granulated sugar

1½ teaspoons dark brown sugar

¼ teaspoon ground cinnamon

⅛ heaping teaspoon cayenne pepper

⅛ heaping teaspoon salt

1   Preheat an oven or toaster oven to 350°F.
    Toss the seeds with the sugars, cinnamon,
    cayenne, and salt.

2   Spread the seeds out on a baking sheet
    lined with aluminum foil and roast for 10
    to 15 minutes, until they are toasted and
    beginning to pop. Midway through the
    cooking, give the pan a shake to help prevent
    sticking. Remove the baking sheet from the
    oven and let the seeds cool. Don't worry if
    there's some sticking; those bits are easy
    enough to remove from the foil and become
    deliciously brittlelike.

OATMEAL COOKIE FRUIT CRISP

serves 6 to 8

6 tablespoons (¾ stick) plus
   1 teaspoon unsalted butter
½-day-old PB&C Oatmeal Skillet
   Cookie (see page 108)
¾ teaspoon ground cinnamon
¼ teaspoon cayenne pepper

¼ teaspoon salt, plus more as
   needed
½ cup plus 1 tablespoon salted
   peanuts
3½ cups blueberries
   (about 18 ounces)

4 cups coarsely chopped peeled
   ripe mango
¼ cup plus 2 tablespoons packed
   dark brown sugar
Zest of 1 lime

If you happened to have an oatmeal cookie lying around, and if you were in a somewhat imaginative frame of mind, you might perceive that baked good as a crisp topping waiting to happen. Or maybe that's just my own zany brand of culinary magical thinking. All I know is that I had a giant PB&C Oatmeal Skillet Cookie in front of me, and the only thing I could think to do with it was strew it over a cast-iron skillet flush with fruit.

1   Preheat the oven to 375°F. In a small saucepan, melt 6 tablespoons of the butter over medium-high heat and set it aside to cool slightly. Crumble the oatmeal cookie into a medium bowl to get a few larger, loose chunks scattered among smaller bits with a few clusters of crumbs here and there. Add the cinnamon, cayenne, and salt to the broken cookie parts and toss them together gently with your hands to combine. Taste and, if necessary, add more salt.

2   Add the peanuts to the bowl and toss to combine. Pour the melted butter over the crumb base and, using a rubber spatula, stir to incorporate, making sure all the crumbs are moistened. Set the topping aside while you make the fruit filling. (If you want to make the topping in advance, place it in a single layer in a baking pan, cover with plastic wrap or aluminum foil, and refrigerate for up to 1 day.)

3   Preheat a 10-inch cast-iron skillet on the stovetop over low heat. Meanwhile, in a large bowl, combine the fruit with the brown sugar and lime zest, stirring to mix.

4   Place the remaining 1 teaspoon butter in the warm skillet to melt, tilting to coat. Turn off the heat and pour the fruit filling into the pan. Add the topping, spreading it out to evenly cover the fruit. Bake for 15 minutes, until the top is brown and crispy. Cover with aluminum foil and bake for 20 minutes more. Serve hot or warm, from the skillet, with vanilla ice cream, crème fraîche, plain frozen yogurt, or whipped cream, sweetened to taste.

TEA-INFUSED STICKY BUN BREAD PUDDING

serves 6

BREAD PUDDING

1½ cups heavy or whipping
   cream

½ cup milk

1 tablespoon plus 2 teaspoons
   loose oolong tea (see Notes)

⅓ cup sugar

6 large egg yolks

½ teaspoon vanilla extract

⅛ teaspoon salt

4 sticky buns, each cubed into
   6 pieces

APRICOT WHIPPED CREAM

1 cup heavy cream

¼ cup crème fraîche or sour
   cream

¼ cup best-quality apricot jam

Stale baguettes, rustic sourdough loaves, or fancier brioches are the default for this breed of "pudding," a baked, custard-soaked bread dish that is usually sweet, but sometimes savory. Croissants, doughnuts, *kouign amanns*, and panettone have all been recruited for extra gut-busting, intensely lush expressions of this humble comfort food. Are sticky buns any more indulgent than those others? When they are Melissa Weller's (page 131), they might be. And should you have any to spare, you're certainly not going to chuck them.

But how to put them in a bread pudding without inducing a nauseating sugar rush or creating something so obscenely rich as to be inedible? I'll tell you how: tea. Its tannins staunch excess sweetness and pair well with baked goods. A topping in the style of chef Nancy Silverton, who folds a jot of crème fraîche into her cold heavy cream, chimes in with a contrasting cooling note. I slip some apricot jam in there, too, for a tart, fruity pucker that, as it happens, is a verified match for fragrant Chinese oolong tea.

1   **Make the bread pudding:** In a small saucepan, warm the cream and milk over low-medium heat. Bring the mixture just below boiling point; when you see little bubbles around the rim of the milk, turn off the heat. Using an infuser or small strainer, submerge the oolong tea into the hot liquid. Cover the saucepan and let the tea steep for at least 45 minutes, until the liquid is cool. Remove and discard the tea. (You can also add the oolong buds directly and pour the infused liquid through a fine-mesh sieve to strain it before incorporating.) Gently warm the infused cream mixture over low heat while you prepare the rest of the custard base.

2   In a large bowl, whisk together the sugar and egg yolks until they're well blended. Slowly add the warm infused cream, whisking constantly to incorporate. Using a fine-mesh sieve, strain the mixture into another bowl and skim off any foam. Add the vanilla and salt and stir to combine.

3   In a large, wide bowl, place the sticky bun cubes and pour the custard over them. Lay a piece of plastic wrap on top of the mixture and put a smaller dish or bowl on top of the plastic wrap to act as a weight to keep the sticky bun cubes submerged in the custard. Add additional weights, such as a stack of even smaller bowls or a large canned item, if necessary. Set it aside to sit for 1 hour, until the cubes are soaked through.

4   Meanwhile, preheat the oven to 325°F with a 10-inch cast-iron skillet placed on a middle rack. Put the mixing bowl and whisk for the whipping cream in the freezer to chill.

5   Fill an ovenproof pan or dish with water and place it on the bottom rack in the oven, and remove the hot skillet. Uncover the soaking cubes and pour them with the custard and any remaining morsels into the cast-iron skillet and cover it with aluminum foil. Using a fork, prick a few holes in the foil to allow steam to escape. Bake it, covered, for 40 minutes.

6   Remove the foil from the skillet and bake for another 15 minutes to let the top brown a bit, without drying out the bread pudding. The buns should looks glossy, with bubbling pockets of melted butter being released.

7   **Meanwhile, make the apricot whipped cream:** Remove the chilled bowl from the freezer and attach to a stand mixer fitted with a whisk, then begin to whip the heavy cream on low speed until it thickens. Raise the speed to medium-high, continuing to whip. Stop the mixer right before the cream is able to hold soft peaks. Remove the bowl from the machine and, using a whisk, finish whipping by hand. (Alternatively, you can whip the cream with a handheld electric mixer or with a whisk entirely by hand. Just make sure your bowl and whisk are cold.) Using a rubber spatula, fold in the crème fraîche followed by the apricot jam.

8   Remove the finished bread pudding from the oven and let it sit in the skillet for a couple of minutes to set before serving it hot in bowls or on plates with a generous dollop or two of the Apricot Whipped Cream.

NOTES

- You can adjust the amount of tea depending on the type and quality of leaves you're using. If you're going with a stronger black tea (a Darjeeling or Earl Grey), a tea with a more pronounced flavor (a fermented Pu-erh or a smoky Lapsang Souchong), or a heavily spiced varietal (Chai), you can use the same quantity. Herbals, like chamomile or rooibos, are weaker so you may need to use more leaves.

- Bread puddings are frequently baked in a bain marie (or water bath) to ensure even cooking with a creamy, moist consistency and a glossy finish. Quick to rust, cast iron can't be subjected to that technique, hence the pan full of water at the bottom of the oven, which generates steam heat.

CONDIMENTS

Opposite: (left) Hot Honey Butter, page 214; (right) My Strawberry Jam!, page 209

GIARDINIERA

makes about 6 cups

¼ head cauliflower

2 shallots

6 garlic cloves

2 carrots

1 cucumber, seeded

1 yellow bell pepper

1 red bell pepper

Leaves from 10 sprigs fresh thyme

1 tablespoon fennel seeds

1 tablespoon crushed red pepper flakes

1 tablespoon plus 1 teaspoon salt

1 cup white vinegar

2 cups olive oil, or more as needed to submerge the vegetables completely

When overachiever Michelle Rizzolo sent me her focaccia recipe (page 142), it arrived with a topping and everything! Giardiniera, she explained, is a spicy, salty Italian accompaniment that can be made with whatever vegetables are readily available. In a two-hour quick-pickling process, salt and vinegar do the seasoning and fermenting; oil does the preserving. I've discovered it tastes great with Charred Green Pea Hummus (page 211) and egg salad (page 196).

1 By hand or using a mandoline, cut the cauliflower florets, shallots, and garlic to ⅛-inch thickness. Julienne the carrots, cucumber, and peppers. In a large nonreactive bowl, combine all the vegetables and toss them with the thyme, fennel seeds, red pepper flakes, salt, and vinegar to thoroughly incorporate. Let the mixture sit for a few hours at room temperature.

2 Strain off the liquid and transfer the drained vegetables to a plastic storage container. Cover them with enough olive oil to submerge. Seal the container and store it in the refrigerator for up to 2 weeks.

PAN-FRIED SAGE PESTO

makes about ½ cup

¼ cup pine nuts

¼ cup olive oil

1 garlic clove

1 cup packed sage leaves

½ teaspoon kosher salt

¼ cup grated Parmesan cheese

¼ cup extra-virgin olive oil

Usually, I know, pesto is made from a raw herb, like basil, or a leafy green (people have been using anything from carrot tops to dandelion greens these days), but sage doesn't perform so well raw; it's bitter. Unless you're using a small amount as a seasoning, you really ought to cook it. Toast the garlic in the oil you're using to pan-fry the herb, then combine it with all the other ingredients to end up with a standout pesto.

1 Preheat a 10-inch cast-iron skillet on the stovetop, gradually raising the heat from low to medium-high. When the pan is hot, add the pine nuts and toast them for about 3 minutes, shaking the pan continuously to move them around, until they start to brown. Quickly take the pan off the stovetop, emptying the pine nuts into a small bowl before they have a chance to burn.

2 Return the pan to the heat and add the olive oil. Once it's hot, add the garlic and cook it for about a minute, flipping it with a wooden spatula every few seconds so each side has a chance to toast and making sure it doesn't burn. Place the toasted garlic in a large mortar (or a food processor) and add the sage leaves to the pan. If the oil begins to spatter heavily, reduce the heat to medium.

3 Using the wooden spatula, stir the sage continuously for about 1½ minutes, so it wilts, darkens, and cooks through without burning or becoming too crisp. It should resemble sautéed spinach. Add the cooked sage to the mortar with the toasted garlic and turn the stove off.

4 Add the salt to the mortar and, using the pestle (or running your food processor), crush the ingredients together to begin to break the garlic and sage down and form a paste. Add the pine nuts, and continue pounding to combine. Do the same with the Parmesan.

5 Slowly incorporate the extra-virgin olive oil, pouring it in a bit at a time and using the pestle to stir and grind it into the paste, which should become thicker and more like a sauce as you continue to add more oil. Store the pesto in a sealed container in the refrigerator for up to 1 week.

CHESTNUT PESTO

makes about 1²/₃ cups

1½ cups whole cooked peeled
    chestnuts
¼ cup grated Parmesan cheese
1 small garlic clove, coarsely
    chopped

Leaves from 4 sprigs fresh thyme
2 large fresh basil leaves
¾ teaspoon flake salt
2 teaspoons balsamic vinegar

¼ cup plus 3 tablespoons extra-
    virgin olive oil
2 tablespoons minced dry sun-
    dried tomatoes

Having become perniciously allergic to walnuts at age seventeen, I can *almost* imagine how Jody Williams's *pesto di noci* tastes. At her gastrothèque Buvette, one of my neighborhood canteens and everyone's idea of the quintessential French wine bar, I longingly watch open-face tartines mounded with a glistening, chunky, amber-colored paste pass by. It looks like a pâté, but it's made of walnuts. They're bound by olive oil, Parmesan, thyme, and, the surprise ingredient, sun-dried tomato. I saw no reason not to try it with crumbly, meaty, starchy-sweet chestnuts—*castagne*. (Those I can eat.) Now I have my own pesto. I'll never know how it compares to the original. I only know I'd happily order it off any menu, and not as a booby prize.

1   Preheat a 10-inch cast-iron skillet on the stovetop, gradually raising the heat from low to medium-high. When the pan is hot, add the chestnuts. Cook for 5 minutes, stirring frequently, to toast and darken the nuts, being careful not to burn them.

2   Transfer them to a food processor. Add the cheese, garlic, thyme, basil, salt, and vinegar and process for a few seconds until you have what resembles a coarse bread crumb mixture. Pour it into a medium bowl and stir in the olive oil and sun-dried tomatoes, mixing to combine and form a thick pesto. Serve it on toast. Stored in a sealed container, it can stay in the refrigerator for up to 1 week.

MY STRAWBERRY JAM!

makes 1½ cups

4 generous cups rinsed and
  hulled strawberries
½ cup sugar
2 tablespoons fresh lemon juice

1 teaspoon rose water
Pinch of salt
5 sprigs fresh tarragon

1 teaspoon freshly cracked black
  pepper (or less, if you want
  less of a kick)

Most experienced preservationists would probably blanch at the thought of making jam in a cast-iron skillet. They would also probably encourage me to do the whole canning thing with the sterilized jars and the airtight sealing. That's not my style. I'm a refrigerator jam kind of girl. I make a small amount, and I store it in my fridge for up to two weeks—it's usually gone before then.

1   Preheat a 10-inch cast-iron skillet on the stovetop, gradually raising the heat from low to medium.

2   Meanwhile, in a medium bowl, combine the strawberries and sugar and, using a potato masher or whatever resourceful version of a masher you've got, mash them together to break down and macerate the berries. Add the lemon juice, rose water, and salt and, using a wooden spoon, stir to combine. While you're at it, you can use the spoon to break apart any strawberry pieces that are too large; you want a chunky jam with bits of fruit in it, but nothing unwieldy.

3   Pour the strawberry mixture into the hot skillet. Add the tarragon. Using the wooden spoon, stir continuously over medium heat for 20 to 25 minutes, until the mixture is bubbling aggressively and, more important, has thickened up. If you drag your spoon through, it should leave a clear trail.

4   Take the pan off the heat and discard the tarragon sprigs. Transfer the mixture to a glass jar and stir in the pepper. Let the jam cool to room temperature, cover it with a lid, and store it in the fridge for up to 2 weeks (though you'll probably eat it a lot faster than that).

The Roman Test

Here's how food editor Alison Roman determines if her jam is ready: Refrigerate a plate before you start the recipe. When you think it's done, spoon some of the cooked fruit onto the cold dish and chill it in the fridge for 5 minutes. The blob should be "slightly jellied." If it's still runny, cook it for another 5 minutes, until it reaches optimal thickness.

CHARRED GREEN PEA HUMMUS

makes about 3 cups

½ cup plus 1 teaspoon
    extra-virgin olive oil
2 (10-ounce) packages frozen
    green peas, thawed and
    patted dry
½ cup tahini

1 small to medium garlic clove
1 scallion (white and light green
    parts), trimmed, halved, and
    split
¼ cup fresh lemon juice

4 large fresh mint leaves
2 teaspoons kosher salt, plus
    more as needed
2 teaspoons chopped fresh
    chives, for garnish

Philadelphia chef Eli Kulp gave me the recipe for the roasted butternut squash hummus he serves at High Street on Market, and I ate that dip like chocolate mousse, by the spoonful. His removal of garbanzos may have been controversial—for some—but he kept the spread's adjunct mainstays: garlic, tahini, lemon juice, and olive oil. I wondered how I could rig a similar outcome using another vegetable. Green peas seemed the most likely to produce comparable results. With a cast-iron pan, I could put some char on them, getting them crispy and brown. Then into the food processor they went. I chucked in fresh mint, scallion, and, as a garnish, chives, which, starting with the necessary garlic, brings your allium tally to three. These additions gave the purée a greater profundity of green flavor to match its gorgeous hue.

1   Preheat a 10-inch cast-iron skillet on the stovetop, gradually raising the heat from low to medium-high. When the pan is hot, add 1 teaspoon of the extra-virgin olive oil and tilt to coat. Add the peas and cook for 15 to 17 minutes, until they've begun to char. Use a wooden spoon or spatula to stir them every couple of minutes so they don't burn and are evenly cooked. Remove the skillet from the heat and let it sit for 10 minutes to cool down a bit.

2   Set aside ¼ cup of the charred peas and place the rest in a food processor. Add the tahini, garlic, scallion, lemon juice, remaining ½ cup olive oil, mint, and salt and purée for a few seconds until you get a smooth, hummuslike consistency. Transfer the mixture to a medium bowl. Stir in the reserved ¼ cup charred peas. Taste and add more salt if necessary. Garnish with the chives. Store the hummus in a sealed container in the refrigerator for 3 to 4 days.

ROASTED EGGPLANT SPREAD
WITH HONEY & NIGELLA

makes 1 cup

1 head of garlic

2 tablespoons olive oil

2 to 3 sprigs fresh thyme, plus
more for garnish

2 small to medium eggplants, or
3 Fairytale eggplants

1 tablespoon plus 1 teaspoon
kosher salt

2 tablespoons plus 1 teaspoon
orange blossom honey (see
Note)

½ teaspoon whole peppercorns
(black, pink, or green)

1 tablespoon nigella seeds

1 teaspoon sherry vinegar

There is another item at Alex Raij and Eder Montero's aforementioned La Vara restaurant that pulled my remix trigger: crisp-battered eggplant batons, sticky with floral honey, sitting on a pungent puddle of creamy, melted cheese, and scattered with nigella seeds, those small, black, slightly acrid grains that taste mostly of onion, with hints of caraway, oregano, and cumin. It's the kitchen's take on a classic Andalusian dish, and it got me thinking about eggplant dip. Roasted garlic's funky sweetness strengthens the connection between the nightshade and the orange blossom honey. Pan-roasted in oil, the garnishing seeds gain in onion aroma as they get nice and toasty. Once stirred into the purée, they disperse firecrackers of crunch throughout the soft pulp. A final, necessary splash of sherry vinegar opens everything up, letting a neon burst of acid in.

1   Preheat the oven to 400°F with a 10-inch cast-iron skillet in it.

2   Slice across the top of the head of garlic to expose the tops of the cloves. Place the head on a square of aluminum foil and drizzle 1 teaspoon of the olive oil over the exposed cloves. Surround the garlic with the thyme sprigs and wrap it up in the foil. Place the garlic bundle in the hot skillet and roast for 40 minutes. The head should be soft enough that you can squeeze the cloves right out of it.

3   While the garlic is roasting, split the eggplants lengthwise. Place the eggplant halves in a large bowl and rub them all over with 1 tablespoon of the salt. Let the eggplants sit for at least 30 minutes (while the garlic roasts).

4   Remove the garlic from the oven and place the aluminum bundle on the countertop to cool. Return the skillet to the oven and reduce the heat to 350°F.

5   Rinse the eggplants thoroughly to remove the salt and pat them dry with an absorbent paper towel or a kitchen towel. Coat each half with ½ teaspoon of the olive oil. Place the oiled eggplant, flesh-side down, in the skillet. Roast for about 30 minutes, until the flesh is soft and mushy.

6   Scoop out the eggplant flesh and place it in a food processor (or a blender), discarding the skin. Purée the flesh until it resembles applesauce. Squeeze the garlic cloves out of their skins into the food processor and process again to combine. Add 2 tablespoons of the honey, the remaining 1 teaspoon salt, and the peppercorns and process to incorporate, stopping when all the peppercorns have been cracked.

7   Transfer the purée to a small serving bowl, and set it aside while you prepare the garnish.

8   The skillet should still be hot from roasting the eggplant; if it isn't (or if you've had to rinse it to remove any residue), preheat it on the stovetop, gradually raising the heat from low to medium-high. Once the pan is hot, add the remaining 1 tablespoon olive oil. When the oil is hot, add the nigella seeds and shake the pan to distribute them across the surface. Fry the seeds in the hot oil for about a minute, until they begin to pop and emit a nutty, toasted odor.

9   Pour the oil and toasted seeds over the top of the eggplant purée. Drizzle it with the vinegar and remaining 1 teaspoon honey. Finally, sprinkle it with fresh thyme leaves. Once it's on the table, stir it up and spoon it onto a torn piece of the flatbread of your choice. Store leftover spread in a sealed container in the refrigerator for 3 to 4 days.

NOTE   You could get muskier with a buckwheat honey, smokier with a chestnut honey, or tangier with pomegranate molasses.

HOT HONEY BUTTER

makes about 1⅓ cups

8 tablespoons (1 stick) unsalted
butter

1 cup orange blossom honey (or
your favorite honey)

2 teaspoons Aleppo pepper or
shichimi togarashi

2 teaspoons flake salt, plus more
as needed

When pastry chef Katzie Guy-Hamilton taught me how to bake a Provençal breakfast bread called *gibassier,* she served it with a thick, whipped-caramel look-alike that was a combination of brown butter, orange blossom honey, and salt. I realized the ridiculously nutty velvety goo could be even more awesome in fiery form. I adapted the recipe for a cast-iron skillet, trying one batch with Aleppo pepper, and another with *shichimi togarashi,* a Japanese seven-spice powder with chiles, sesame seeds, and dried orange peel. You should take as many liberties as you like: Add more or less fire, to your taste, or, even change the heat source with your own ground dried chile mix. And slather with abandon—on flatbreads, on biscuits, on cornbread, on *gibassiers,* on everything.

1   Preheat a 10-inch cast-iron skillet on the stovetop, gradually raising the heat from low to medium. Once the pan is hot, add the butter, tilting to coat. As it melts, it will sizzle and foam. Cook it until the foam dissolves and the butter turns the color of hazelnut, a rich brown. (Make sure it doesn't burn.) If it's spattering too much, reduce the heat a bit.

2   Once the butter is brown, immediately add the honey, stirring vigorously with a wooden spoon or spatula, for about a minute, starting in the center and swirling outward, to thoroughly incorporate. Bring the mixture to a boil and let it cook for a minute more; it will bubble and foam rather dramatically.

3   Remove from the heat and pour it straight into a blender. Pulse for a few seconds so it emulsifies and is glossy and grease-free. Pour it into a bowl, and while it's still hot, whisk in the Aleppo to combine. Add the salt and whisk again to incorporate. Taste and adjust the seasoning as needed.

4   Let the sauce sit for 10 minutes to infuse. Serve immediately or place in a sealed container, let cool completely, and refrigerate for up to 3 weeks.

CHOCOSTACHIO SPREAD

makes 1⅓ cups

1 cup shelled raw pistachio nuts

¼ cup best-quality unsweetened cocoa powder

¼ cup sugar

1 teaspoon vanilla extract

¼ teaspoon kosher salt

2 tablespoons canola oil

½ cup plus 2 tablespoons mascarpone

My friend Sierra perfectly articulated my thoughts about this reinterpretation of Nutella when, after taking a spoonful, she said, "It tastes like brownie batter!" It really does, and I like it on toast—buttered brioche or olive oil–drizzled country bread—with some strawberry jam, or old-school booze-soaked cherries (Luxardo maraschinos, ideally). Also encouraged: dipping shortbread cookies into it or daubing it onto a freshly baked, split biscuit to make a filled sandwich.

1 Preheat a 10-inch cast-iron skillet on the stovetop, gradually raising the heat from low to medium. When the pan is hot, add the pistachios and cook the nuts for 3 to 4 minutes, stirring with a wooden spoon or spatula, until they exude a pronounced toasted smell.

2 Transfer the toasted pistachio nuts to a food processor. Let them sit for 5 to 10 minutes to cool down a bit so they're not too hot. Process the nuts for 2½ to 3 minutes until they form a paste. Stop the machine midway through processing to smooth and, using a rubber spatula, scrape down the sides of the food processor bowl. Add the cocoa powder, sugar, vanilla, salt, and canola oil and process for up to 90 seconds to get a smooth, integrated, thick spread, scraping down the sides of the bowl in the middle of processing, if necessary.

3 Transfer the chocolate-pistachio mixture to a medium bowl. Add the mascarpone and, using a rubber spatula, fold it into the spread until it's thoroughly incorporated. It will keep in the refrigerator, in a sealed container, for 2 weeks, at least.

THE SKILLET PANTRY

One of the most rewarding aspects of writing this book was that it gave me an excuse to play around with different kinds of flours, sugars, and fats. They've become integral to my baking and are now staples in my kitchen. I hope you're equally won over by them. Here are my favorite brands and sources.

FLOUR

Anson Mills | ansonmills.com
Buckwheat flour, cornmeal (coarse and fine), rye flour

Blue Star Brand, Koda Farms | kodafarms.com
Mochiko (sweet rice) flour

Bob's Red Mill | bobsredmill.com
Barley flour, coconut flour, corn flour, garbanzo bean (chickpea) flour, graham (whole-wheat pastry) flour, green pea flour, kamut flour, quinoa flour, semolina flour, sorghum flour, tapioca flour

Buon Italia | buonitalia.com
Double zero ("00") flour

Dowd & Rogers | dowdandrogers.com
Chestnut flour

Kalustyan's | kalustyans.com
Semolina (coarse)

King Arthur | kingarthurflour.com
All-purpose bleached and unbleached flour, bread flour

SWEETENERS

Blis | blisgourmet.com
Grade B maple syrup

Dutch Gold | dutchgoldhoney.com
Buckwheat honey and orange blossom honey (if not locally sourced)

The Date Lady | ilovedatelady.com
Date syrup

Bob's Red Mill
Coconut sugar

Kalustyan's
Pomegranate molasses

FATS

Artisana Organics | artisanaorganics.com
Coconut butter, coconut oil

D'Artagnan | dartagnan.com
Duck fat

Heirloom Provisions | heirloomprovisions.com
Lard (regular or leaf—if not from your local butcher)

Purity Farms | purityfarms.com
Ghee

SPICES, SEASONINGS & OTHER STAPLES

Jacobsen Salt Co. | jacobsensalt.com
Flake sea salt

Kalustyan's
Curry powder, garam masala

La Boîte | laboiteny.com
Za'atar

Nielsen-Massey | nielsenmassey.com
Almond extract, coffee extract

See Smell Taste | seesmelltaste.com
Aleppo pepper, ras el hanout, saffron, Sichuan peppercorns, shichimi togarashi, vanilla bean

Sonoma Syrup | sonomasyrup.com
Vanilla bean extract "crush"

Askinosie | askinosie.com
Cocoa nibs

June Taylor Jams | junetaylorjams.com
Fruit conserves and marmalade

Local Asian grocers
Pagoda Shaoxing rice cooking wine

Love 'n Bake via King Arthur
Almond paste, pistachio paste

Té Company | te-nyc.com
Oolong tea

Panatea | panateamatcha.com
Matcha green tea powder

Valrhona | valrhona-chocolate.com
Baking chocolate (dark, dulcey blond, milk)

Whole Foods
Kefir, labneh (if not locally found in gourmet shop)

ACKNOWLEDGMENTS

When I first asked Caroline Fidanza about the naan she bakes at Saltie, she told me she'd stolen the recipe from a cookbook called *Flatbreads and Flavors*, written by Jeffrey Alford and Naomi Duguid. That's what the history of cooking is, a series of thefts. What elevates each act of stealing to something noncriminal and original are the seemingly small but significant adjustments every person makes along the way. Because of Caroline's adaptations, it's hard to see the resemblance between those two recipes. I'd like to take this opportunity to confess, thank, and note every writer and chef whose recipes, restaurant dish, or advice I drew on for inspiration and know-how:

Jeffrey Alford and Naomi Duguid (duh); Caroline Fidanza (double duh); Lauren Crabbe and Michael McCrory of Andytown Coffee Roasters; Rocky "Super Fry Bread" Yazzie; chef Devon Gilroy and his sous chef Gemma Kaminkorn; the pastry chefs and bakers who went above and beyond, including Pichet Ong, Melissa Weller, Justin Gellatly, Michelle Rizzolo, Gina DePalma, and Gillian Shaw; mistress of Southern baking Lisa Donovan; Atlanta baking legend and cast-iron skillet hoarder Liz Lorber; Hill-of-the-Hawk Heather Lanier; pastry cook Anna Higham; Memphis chefs Michael Hudman and Andy Ticer of Hog & Hominy (home of the best pie on earth); Liz Quijada of Abraço; pastry chef Katzie Guy-Hamilton; Amanda Hesser and her mom; food science expert and patient explainer Harold McGee; chef Eli Kulp; chef Heidi Trull; craftsman William Werner; shortbread queen Caitlin Freeman; know-it-all Alison Roman; food blogger Molly Yeh and her great aunt-in-law Ethel Ramstead; food blogger Alia Alkasami and her grandmother; food blogger Maya Sozer; chefs Alex Raij and Eder Montero; chef Jody Williams; chef Marc Vetri; chef Brandon Jew; Cathy "Butter Mochi" Juhn via *Lucky Peach* magazine; blogger and pastry chef David Lebovitz; The Recipe Machine (a.k.a. Melissa Clark); Martha Stewart; The Food Lab's Kenji López-Alt; David Arnold; Martha Rose Shulman; food writer Felicity Cloake; Best Made Company's resident cast-iron resuscitator Nick Zdon; chef Mark Ladner; chef Anne Rosenzweig; Ritz-Cookie Tosi; chef Nancy Silverton; pastry chef Shuna Lydon; jamstress June Taylor; *fika* enthusiast Kristin D. Murray; pastry chef Phoebe Lawless; chef Asha Gomez; my local dosa guide Nalini Periasamy; NYC's Levain Bakery; Standard Baking Company; supper club superstar Sabrina Ghayour; chef Maria Elia; Emiko Davies; chef Tom Norrington-Davies; and The Cookbook Squad: The Joneses, Maida Heatter, Shirly O. Corriher, Dorie Greenspan (hi, Dorie!), Alice Medrich, Nick Malgieri, Simon Hopkinson, Nancy Harmon Jenkins (and her daughter chef Sara Jenkins), Yotam Ottolenghi and Sami Tamimi, Paula Wolfert, Virginia Willis, Belinda Ellis, Madhur Jaffrey, Julee

Russo (and Sheila Lukins), Bill Smith, Jim Lahey, Ruta Kahate, Sean Brock, Kristen Miglore, and Marciel E. Presilla.

Mom and Dad, thank you for your support, all the cooking and feeding, and the cookbooks in your kitchen. I am so lucky to have you. Love you. Bro, thanks for checking in along the way.

Lily Freedman, I couldn't have done this without you. Sorry about the celery and anchovies.

To the DREAM TEAM: Aubrie Pick, I wish I could take a photograph that could convey how extraordinary you are and what a joy to work with. Just please know how much I appreciate you, your incredible talent and versatility, and every shot you took for this cookbook. Bessma Khlaef and Courtney Munna, that shoot couldn't have happened without you. Maeve Sheridan, you're the best prop stylist I've ever worked with.

Mike Whitehead, the smartest thing I did was buy a Finex skillet for myself, because it prompted me to track you down. Thank you for your wealth of cast-iron knowledge and your friendship.

Angelin Borsics, thank you for showing me that the cookbook experience doesn't have to be hellish, that it can be fun and wonderfully collaborative. Stephanie Huntwork, you really listened and took all of my requests, stacks of books, and random scraps of information into account; then you turned it all into something so much better than I could have imagined. Doris Cooper, thanks for tea at Cognac and everything else that's followed. Aaron Wehner, thank you for your omniscience, and for the opportunity. And to the behind-the-scenes crew at Potter—Joyce Wong, Heather Williamson, Natasha Martin, Lauren Velasquez, Sonia Persad, and Alexandria Martinez—thanks for doing all that heavy lifting. Laura Nolan, we finally got it right! Thank you for keeping the faith and not letting me throw in the kitchen towel.

Beth Kracklauer, if you hadn't given that stovetop cast-iron story the green light, I would not have typed any of the words on this or the preceding pages.

To my fellow food writers and editors I call "friend," thank you, so much, for your support, advice, and championing. To my non-food-world-specific friends: all the love, respect, and gratitude.

Pawstein, kisses.

INDEX